This memoir is dedicated to my adoptive parents
Anna and Karl Wentersdorf
who, with their love and caring,
gave me a second chance at life some 74 years ago.

Born in the Year Zero

A Memoir of Struggle and Renewal

Tony Wentersdorf

Born in the Year Zero
A Memoir of Struggle and Renewal
by Tony Wentersdorf
©2020

Printed in the United States of America
First Printing, September 2020

ISBN 978-1-63649-509-5

Tony Wentersdorf
1350 Nicollet Mall, Apartment 607
Minneapolis, MN 55403
afwentersdorf@hotmail.com

I would like to thank all those who helped me bring
this memoir to fruition, including Tom Cassidy who assembled
and formatted this book for print, Steve Wentworth for
his tech support, and Christa Seiler and numerous other friends
for their encouragement and positive testimonials.

Musical Comedy Editions ◆ Minneapolis ◆ Portland OR

PREFACE

This memoir is divided into three sections: *Born in the Year Zero, Growing Up in America*, and *At Home and Abroad*.

Part I describes the years of my life from my birth in 1945 in Marburg, Germany, to my early abandonment, adoption, and subsequent life in various German towns. It concludes with my emigration to the U.S. with my dad at the age of nine. I titled it *Born in the Year of Zero* because 1945 (referred to as *Die Stunde Null – The Hour Zero*) marks the low point in modern German history.

Part Ii describes my childhood and adolescence from the time my dad and I moved to Cincinnati, Ohio when I was nine years old, up to the time I started college as an undergraduate at the age of nineteen. It traces my life from parochial schools, to junior and senior high school, ending with my first year at Xavier University.

Part Iii tells the mostly chronological story of my adult years, beginning with my coming of age at Xavier University, my graduate year at Ohio State, and my travels and stays abroad in Paris, Zurich, and Marburg from 1968 to 1973. I also include stories of my life in Minnesota, beginning in 1974. There are chapters on falling in love for the first time, my discovery of the autoharp, my struggles with mental illness, my beginnings as a storyteller, my love of baseball, and my discovery of a new spiritual home.

In reconstructing the events of my life, I often found it difficult to distinguish my own memories from the stories my dad or others told me, especially during my life in Germany and my early years in Cincinnati. I don't always recall the exact things that were said, but I try to stay true to the gist of what happened.

Writing this memoir has been invaluable experience because it enabled me to reconstruct important events in my life and make sense of things I often didn't understand at the time. I owe my dad and others I interviewed an invaluable debt for chronicling early childhood events that I don't remember.

Part One: Born in the Year Zero — 9

Part Two: Growing Up in America — 37

Part Three: At Home and Abroad — 75

PART I
Born in the Year Zero

ABANDONED

Babies from a foreign land
Stare at you with empty eyes,
Past their bars and prison cots
Where they rock away their lives.

Babies from a foreign land,
Crammed like sardines into rooms
With no toys and with no hope,
Strangle slowly in their tombs.

Babies from a foreign land,
Changed and fed with clock-work pace,
Craving to be held and touched,
Look for love in every face.

Babies from a foreign land
Never whimper, never rest,
Got no mommies and got no dads,
Never taste a mother's breast.

I – From Abandonment to Adoption

I was born Raimund Hofeditz on Tuesday August 7th 1945 in Marburg an der Lahn, Germany. I never got to know my biological parents because my unmarried birth mother - Hildegard - placed me in a Marburg orphanage run by the Diakonissen Schwestern (Deaconness nuns), when I was just a few days old. I stayed there for about eighteen months until the winter of 1947. Of course, I have no memories of that time. The only things I know are what my adopting father told me much later when I was in my early twenties.

According to my adoptive dad, the orphanage was overcrowded and understaffed since I was admitted there at the end of World War II when things were pretty chaotic in Germany. It was a time of great privation and hunger during which lots of refugees were fleeing the bombed out larger cities like Hamburg, Berlin, Munich, and Frankfurt to smaller towns and villages which hadn't suffered as much from the bombings. My birthplace, Marburg, for example, suffered only minor damage.

Not only was the orphanage overcrowded and understaffed, but a lot of the infants there were of mixed race – born of African-American GIs and German women, and subsequently abandoned because of the shame surrounding mixed-race births. I was one of the few white babies.

When I was about a year old, I contracted diphtheria, became critically ill, and had to be hospitalized. However, this hospitalization was a blessing in disguise because it may have saved my life by providing me with enough touch, care, and attention to survive. Otherwise, I probably would have died of a "failure to thrive." By the time I returned to the orphanage from the hospital, I was able to recover from my illness without major long term physical effects except that I remained anemic and undernourished. Because I wasn't held much in the orphanage, I developed chronic skin problems. I also had problems swallowing solid food since I subsisted mainly on a diet of milk and porridge. Shortly after returning to the orphanage from the hospital, I got a visit from a poor young married couple named Anna Jankowski and Karl Wentersdorf.

Karl was born in a little town in the Eastern part of Germany, in what is now Poland. When he was two years old his father was killed in combat during World War I. His mother was an English teacher who sent him to London when he was about eight years old so he could become fluent in English. There he lived with a couple of aunts. But when he reached puberty, he had increasing difficulties in getting on with them because they didn't know how to handle a teenage boy. So, when he was fifteen, they sent him back to Berlin to live with his mother. He stayed there until he became an adult and moved out to get his own apartment to start working.

During the war he was spared from being sent into combat because he had a severe back problem called spondylitis which made walking very painful. For a while he even had to use a cane. Even though he was never a party member and despised the Nazis, he worked for Intelligence listening in and translating BBC broadcasts, and intercepting American communications with the Soviets to learn about troop movements. For example, he heard Edward R. Murrow report from North Africa and the Eastern Front.

Anna was born in St. Petersburg, Russia in 1899 of German-Polish parents. While she was growing up, she had a chance to study in France and England. As a result, she became fluent in five languages: Russian, Polish, German, French, and English. However, around the time of the Russian Revolution in 1917, she had to flee the Soviet Union with her widowed mother, *Babuschka*, and her two sisters Lucie and Elsa. They all settled in Berlin. There Anna and Lucie worked for a while as script girls for UFA, the German movie industry. Eventually, she used her language skills to start a translation business called AKATE. Her work there consisted in translating business and technical correspondence into German. Karl, who was fifteen years younger, became one of her employees sometime in the mid-thirties. Later on they ran the translation business together. Soon they fell in love and eventually got married at the end of World War II.

When their Berlin home was destroyed in the day-and-night bombings during the war, Karl and Anna fled to Marburg. It is a small town in the North-Central part of Western Germany, about 50 kilometers north of

Frankfurt. They were drawn to Marburg because it was only slightly damaged during the war. My dad was also eager to settle there because it had a well-known university where he could pursue his interest in Shakespeare. He got to know one of the English professors there, Dr.Heinrich Mutschmann, who was a well-known Shakespeare scholar and soon became his mentor. Because Karl didn't have the resources to study at the university, he worked with Professor Mutschmann privately.

By the time Anna and Karl arrived in Marburg, they had little more than the clothes on their backs, a small suitcase with some valuables, and Anna's precious typewriter which she managed to salvage. Soon many of the American occupation forces in Marburg hired them to translate important documents and correspondence. Because of Karl's bi-lingual knowledge of English and German, plus Anna's command of five languages, they both proved invaluable to the Americans. Not only could Anna translate and speak five languages fluently, she could also do stenography in each. At first, they were hired to translate correspondence and important documents into English. However, they were soon hired to work for the CIC (Counter-Intelligence Corps) to do interpreter work. I remember my dad telling me that my mom once did the interpreting for some American Intelligence officials who were interviewing a top-level Russian general who had defected from the Soviet Union at the end of the war.

In Marburg Karl and Anna got to know a Catholic priest and chaplain named *Pfarrer* Josef Albinger. Father Albinger had survived four years in Dachau concentration camp where he was sent after one of his parishioners turned him in to the Gestapo for preaching against Hitler's euthanasia policy. He would often visit the orphanage where I was staying. He urged Karl and Anna to adopt me since I was one of the few good-looking, white, relatively healthy infants with no major physical problems. At first they were hesitant to adopt because they were barely earning enough to live on, much less take on someone else's baby. But when Anna first saw me there in that crib, rocking back and forth silently, her heart went out to me. I think what clinched her decision to adopt was when, during one of her visits, I reached up to touch her face, and brought her hand to my forehead. My dad thought I may have made this gesture because I had been so used to the hospital nurses taking my temperature.

Once Anna's mind was made up to adopt me, she soon persuaded Karl to do so. Even though I was already about eighteen months old by that time, I could neither walk, talk, crawl, or even make any babbling sounds. My new parents now embarked on the long, tedious, complicated adoption process which involved filling out numerous forms, waiting for months, and jumping over all kinds of other bureaucratic hoops. My adoption finally became official in September 1948, about a year after they first saw me in the orphanage. Fortunately, their staff allowed my parents to take me out of the orphanage to live with them before my adoption became official. Thus, my new life began on a very positive note.

II – New Parents in Wershausen

When Anna and Karl Wentersdorf made the huge decision to adopt me, they were confronted with a tremendous task. Since I could neither walk, talk, chew solid food, nor was potty-trained, I had to learn all these skills in my new parents' home.

And their own situation at the time wasn't the best. They weren't able to find any permanent housing in Marburg, which was already over-crowded with refugees, so they had to find somewhere else to live. Fortunately, through his translation work, my new dad met a young farmer who lived in a small village near Marburg called Wershausen whose mother was willing to take in my parents and me.

Therefore, around the winter of 1947 when I was around eighteen months old, my new parents and I moved into a small two-story farmhouse in Wershausen that was owned by the Stey family. I now received my new adoptive name of Antonius Wentersdorf. The Steys kept chickens and a few pigs on their farm which also had some fruit trees so they could make home-made jam which you couldn't buy in the stores. While Frau Stey lived downstairs with her children, we were given a room upstairs where we were made to feel welcome. Around this time, a poor, roving photographer took some pictures of me and my mom in exchange for food. These are the only pictures I have of me and my new mom. I was about eighteen months old at the time and had curly blonde hair like her.

Around the time my adoption papers were finalized in September 1948, my parents were already working for the Americans. Since the American military headquarters were located in downtown Marburg, they had to walk about seven kilometers to and from their office each day. Thus they had little time to take care of me. Fortunately, Frau Stey was willing to take up the slack and babysit me while they were gone. Not long after we moved into our new Wershausen, home, the military government ordered all young children to be vaccinated. My dad recalled taking me to a school in Marburg where the vaccinations took place. He noticed that as soon as we neared the school, I became very agitated, and started screaming at the top of my lungs. At first, my dad couldn't figure out what was going on, and took me home, figuring it must have been a diaper safety pin stuck in my skin. As soon as we left the school, I stopped crying. But when he tried taking me there a second time, I started screaming again. He finally figured out that the strong smell of ether coming from the school must have triggered a traumatic memory of my stay in the hospital where I must have been given multiple shots. To this day, I hate hypodermic needles!

According to my dad, I was quickly able to adapt to life in the Stey household during the next couple of years. My only direct memory of that time was watching the long yellow strip of sticky flypaper that hung from their kitchen ceiling. I was mesmerized by the many black flies that were stuck there, and couldn't figure out why they didn't fly away.

I now had to be taught how to eat solid foods. This presented a real problem since I had been fed only bottle milk and thin porridge in the orphanage. I had an especially hard time chewing and swallowing meat. I would store an ever growing lump of partly chewed meat inside my mouth in a kind of pouch, sort of like a squirrel storing nuts, instead of swallowing it. That made ingesting more food very difficult.

My mom and dad also bought me my first pair of shoes so I could learn to walk. And when they wondered if I would ever speak or make any sounds, a wise old neighbor lady told them not to worry: "It won't be long before he'll be talking your ear off." And her prediction came true because, once I did start talking, it was with entire words. I finally learned to walk and talk when I was about three years old, and from then on became an active little toddler. My dad later told me that some of my first words were: "Autos, lauter autos." (Cars, many cars.) This was significant because so few people could afford to own cars at that time. So, seeing my first car was a momentous occasion for me. Around this time, my dad bought an apple tree that was one of many fruit trees being auctioned off by the Wershausen mayor, so that people could have the fresh fruit that was still not available in the stores. My dad used the apples, and blackberries we picked in the nearby woods, to make home-made jam. Towards the beginning of 1948, stores finally began stocking common foods and other needed goods. This was helped up by the currency reform of 1948 in which all bank accounts were frozen, so that 1000 old Reichmarks (RM) now became 100 new Deutschmarks (DM). Furthermore, every adult with a bank account was given an initial sum of 50 DM to get started.

Not only did my parents have to walk the seven kilometers from Wershausen to their Marburg office each day, but my dad's spondylitis made walking extremely difficult. When his American employers found out about his condition, they arranged to find a home for him in Marburg, so he didn't have to walk so far. As part of the new de-

Nazification program, the occupation forces appropriated the homes of former high-ranking Nazis. My family was given one of these, a roomy two-story house in the center of Marburg, where I would spend the next year.

MARBURG TOWN

I was born in a little town, Marburg is its name,
Nestled in the hills of Hessenland,
I can see your spires grand, your castle in the dawn,
Your ivied halls and winding river Lahn.
Town of my birth, you're so far away,
In another country – Western Germany.
But it's you where my heart returns whenever I'm alone,
Marburg Town, you're still my home.
Once upon a time, knights rode your cobbled lanes,
And courted fair maidens on their steeds.
In narrow little shops, burghers plied their trades,
And men like Luther carved your history.
It wasn't long ago when tanks rolled down your streets,
Many thousands suffered hunger and great pain,
Yet you survived it all, and lived to tell the tale,
Brought new life from the ashes of the slain.
You showed me another way when I was feeling lost,
To make new friends and find my roots again,
You gave me back my life and loving family,
You helped me join the old times with the new.

III – Family Reunion in Marburg

Although our move to Marburg was a positive thing since my dad no longer had to walk the seven kilometers to and from work each day, a new problem presented itself. Who would take care of me while my parents were working since Frau Stey was no longer able to do it? Fortunately this problem was solved when my grandmother Babuschka,

her sister, *Tante* (Aunt) Lucie, and Lucie's daughter Ali were able to move in with us in our large new Marburg home.

Like my mom and dad, Babuschka, Lucie, Elsa and Ali had lived in Berlin during the thirties after they had fled Russia. However, after Lucie had a baby girl, she and her mother were sent, first to the German-speaking part of Czechoslovakia (Sudetenland), and later to Bavaria. This was ordered by the Nazi regime so that young mothers could raise as many kids as possible. And they didn't consider Berlin to be a safe place because of the bombings. Eventually, Babuschka,Tante Lucie, and Ali moved to Marburg to be re-united with my mom who was Lucie's sister. By the time Lucie arrived in Marburg , her daughter Ali was four years old, about a year older than me.

From now on, Tante Lucie was able to take care of me and her daughter. She also did the cooking, cleaning, and other household chores, while my mom and dad were at work. My dad told me that I was a quiet, good-natured boy who adapted well to my new home, and got on well with my cousin Ali. I don't remember much about that time except playing in the sand with Ali along the banks of the Lahn River which flowed through the town. I loved the water even then.

 Once we got settled in our new home in Marburg, my dad built me a small sandbox of which I still have a picture in a photo album my dad made for me. In fact, my dad loved to take lots of pictures with his new Vogtlander camera that he bought once his economic situation improved. Around this time, he also started pursuing his Shakespeare studies with his new mentor Dr. Mutschmann. Together they eventually wrote a book in English entitled *Shakespeare and Catholicism*.

I still remember meeting Dr. Mutschmann's wife who often accompanied Dr. Mutschmann to my dad's parties. I avoided her as much as I could because I was afraid of her stern demeanor. I don't remember much about Dr. Mutschmann himself except he was somewhat remote and formal. One of my mother's hobbies was reading murder mysteries. She especially loved Agatha Christie, and my dad was sure to buy her a new mystery for every anniversary. My dad also stayed in touch with Pfarrer Albinger who became our regular pastor.

Even though my living situation improved during my stay in Marburg, and I was eating better, I was still undernourished, and anemic. Therefore, my parents decided to send me to an *Erholungsheim* (convalescent home) for toddlers in a small town in the Southern (Baden-

Wuertemberg) part of Germany called Buchau/Federsee . I stayed there during the summer of 1950. Even though I don't remember any of this, I still have a photo of me on an excursion with some other kids. I can tell from the photo that I was a bit older than most of the toddlers.

After I came back from the convalescent home a few months later, my health continued to improve. My dad told me that when he and my mom picked me up at the train station, I was singing a popular children's song in the Swabian dialect called *Auf de schwaeb'sche Eisebahn* (On the Swabian Train). This children's song describes all the different stops the train makes, and describes the various passengers – all in dialect. That was the first time I showed an interest in music. And as soon as we got seated in the street car on our way home, I surprised my mom by telling her: *"Du bist eine schoene Dame."* (You are a beautiful lady.)

Unfortunately, however, my mom became seriously ill around this time. At first, the doctors weren't able to diagnose the problem, but eventually they discovered it was ovarian cancer. By the time her illness was diagnosed, it was too late to operate because it had spread to her other organs. The doctor advised my father not to tell her she had cancer because that's the way medicine was practiced in those days. But she suspected something was wrong, and asked him one day soon after her diagnosis: *"Ist es krebs?"* (Is it cancer?) When he was unable to answer, she got very angry. She was also mad at her doctor for not telling her the truth, or at least offering her some hope for a cure.

Around this time, she had gotten wind of some miraculous new remedy that was supposed to cure cancer. It involved ingesting extracts from the parasitic shrub mistletoe. This experimental, highly suspect treatment was frowned upon by most of the doctors they consulted, but it was being used by a private hospital in Stuttgart, a city in Southern Germany. So, undeterred by the high cost, my mom insisted on going there. She persuaded her American supervisors to drive her to Stuttgart free of charge. But her health insurance wouldn't cover her treatment because it was considered a quack cure. Therefore, my dad had to dip into his savings to pay for her lengthy hospital stay. Throughout this ordeal, her hope for a miracle cure never wavered until the end when became obvious she wasn't getting any better.

My dad managed to visit her whenever he could get time off from work. I remember him telling me that during one of his final visits, she asked him again: "Ist es Krebs?" He still wasn't able to tell her the truth, but broke down crying instead. Then she knew that the situation was hopeless. But she still asked him to smuggle in cigarettes because she had always been a chain smoker. He knew that doing this would just hasten her death, but he didn't have the heart to deny her this last pleasure. My mom died on January 24, 1951, not long after her fifty-first birthday. She was buried in Stuttgart.

The only ones attending her funeral were my dad and Tante Lucie. He didn't take me along. Although I don't remember him telling me of her death, I must have sensed something was wrong when she didn't return from the hospital, and I never saw her again. I still have a small photo taken of me around this time in which I look very sad.

In spite of her tragic death, my mom did leave me with a lasting legacy, which made me realize how much she loved me. When I was in my fifties, my dad sent me copies of two letters she wrote to me on her death bed. When I read those letters and realized her feelings towards me, I broke down crying. I translated them into English, and will always treasure her final words to me. The first of these was written shortly after her birthday in December 1950.

"Dearest son, my heart, my Antoscha! This letter is once more for you, just for you alone! I thank you very much for your nice gift for my birthday: for the lovely soft handkerchiefs, the dear little, funny candle shaped like a mushroom, and for your birthday card. On the card is written: 'Heartfelt greetings for your birthday from your Toni.' And on the card is drawn a small boy who looks like my son Antoscha, but he is dressed like *Haenschen Klein* and will probably wander the wide world.

"Dearest Tony, I have kissed your birthday card many times…. And thanks for your lovely photos in your snowsuit (in your pictures you are looking directly into my eyes. But you've drawn mostly the naughty things you've done. But I've seen with my Mama's eyes all the good things you've done. That's always made me very happy! I've cut out your little hands which Papa drew for me and have saved them. Now, I have to say goodbye, dearest Tony. Today I've written you two whole pages. I kiss you often, Antoscha – on your mouth, on your cheeks, on your neck, and on both your hands. I hope they are nice and clean and not too raw -- Your Mama Ninka."

About three weeks later, shortly before her death, she wrote her last letter to me in which she bid me a final goodbye. "These are greetings just for you alone, my dear son, Antoscha. I'm sorry, my poor little rabbit, that you became sick on Christmas Day, of all things. I had measles too when I was small and had to lie in bed in a darkened room for fourteen days.

"When it's very dark and you and Papa are sleeping soundly, my soul will visit you. And it will kiss you and dear Papa; it will stroke you, tickle you a bit for fun, and give you beautiful dreams. But my soul can only visit you when you are strong again, when you've been thinking about me with all your might, and when you have wished for my recovery with all your heart. Now I have to say goodbye for today, my dearest loving son.

"I kiss you lovingly on your mouth, dearest, on your hairs, on your slender neck, on your chest, there where your heart beats. Sleep well tonight. Perhaps my soul will visit you then. Your one and only Mama."

Unfortunately, the only direct memory I have of my mom is when she asked me to fold my clothes neatly on a chair before going to bed. But her two letters were a treasure I will never forget. And I'm very grateful to my father for sending them to me. I later wrote a song commemorating those two precious letters:

A LETTER TO MY MOTHER

Dear, mother I am answering the letters that you wrote me
When I was only five years old.
I never got to see them until you were long-gone,
But their words did touch my soul.
You said how much you loved me, your soul would come and see me,
When I was sad and lonely, and kiss me in my sleep.
I was your little Haenschen, you were my warmth and comfort,
Until the day you passed away.
And now I often wonder what things might have been like
If you were still alive today.
Would you tell me about your sleigh rides back in Russia,
Your favorite dog named Tommy, and how things were back then?
I know I'll always miss you though I never knew you,
And we'll never meet again.
Your letters were the treasure that made me cry full measure,
And helped to ease my loss and pain.

IV – A New Home and a New Loss

Around the time of my mom's hospitalization and death, my dad had to move again because his American employers transferred him to another safe house in a small town about thirty kilometers South of Marburg called Giessen-Wieseck. This house had been appropriated by the American Forces, so that the former owner who had been the town's Nazi mayor during the thirties and the war, no longer owned it. However, he was still able to live there with his wife and son. But my dad now became the official caretaker of the property, responsible for maintaining the house and yard. The mayor's wife, Frau Euler, turned out to be very friendly and helpful. She and my dad got on quite well.

Her son Arnold, who was fifteen years younger than my dad, became a good friend. They shared a common love of opera. Since Arnold had a pleasant voice, they spent a lot of time listening to and singing their favorite opera arias from Puccini, Verdi, and Wagner. My dad also coached him in Italian pronunciation since most of the operas they listened to were in Italian. Eventually, my dad sponsored Arnold when he emigrated to the U.S. in 1957.

Since Tante Lucie was no longer able to take care of me in my new home in Giessen-Wieseck, my dad hired a housekeeper named Elizabeth, who took care of me while my dad was at work. She also did the cooking, cleaning, and other household chores.

I have some vivid memories of that house and its yard. I remember that the family owned some chickens and a pig. Once in spring or summer, they slaughtered the pig and some chickens. After Frau Euler cut off the chicken's head, it spent about a minute running around the yard headless, blood spurting from its neck in fountains of bright red. The butchering of the pig was a big deal because they used every part of it for meat and sausages. Even the pig's intestines didn't go to waste because they were used to wrap the sausages in. I loved eating the freshly cooked *Blutwurst* (blood sausage).

Even though I really missed my mom, especially at first, I really liked Elizabeth. She was a young single woman in her early twenties who was engaged to be married. She became like a surrogate mom to me, so much so that some of the neighbor kids thought she was my real mom when she would call me in for dinner after I'd been playing in the yard. One of my favorite things to do at the time was to go swimming. I have one picture of me as a skinny little five year old in my swimming trunks, standing on the landing at the rear of the house with a Elizabeth and another kid, grinning from ear to ear.

But not all my memories were happy ones. I really missed my mom, especially at night. I was very scared of the dark. While my mom was still alive, I used to sleep in the same room with her and my dad. But now that she was gone, my dad tried to get me to be more independent by having me sleep alone in a small room upstairs while he stayed in the downstairs bedroom. I didn't like this new arrangement at all! I would often have terrible nightmares in which I was being chased by monsters and evil gremlins. When I closed my eyes, they would creep up next to my bed to threaten to devour me. But I was also afraid to keep my eyes open because they would still come after me. They often hid underneath my bed where they waited to entrap me as soon as I opened my eyes. I tried to protect myself by imagining that my body was getting bigger and bigger, so big that they wouldn't bother me. But that didn't work too well.

One night I got so scared that I crept downstairs to my dad's bedroom in the middle of the night and begged to sleep in his bed. But he admonished me by saying: "You're a big boy now and need to sleep in your own bed."

Shortly after moving into our new home, I started first grade in Giessen-Wieseck. I don't recall ever attending Kindergarten. The German custom for children starting school was for parents to give them a *Zuckertuete* –a large, colorful, cone-shaped cardboard bag filled with candy, chocolate, and other sweets– to make the start of school more palatable. I still have a photo of me holding my Zuckertuete, with my black leather *schulranzen* (school satchel) on my back, and wearing my brand new brown *lederhosen* (leather shorts). These Lederhosen were held up by a crossed pair of leather suspenders clasped together in the middle by a kind of broche. Even though they were a deer-colored brown when new, they soon turned bright black since I wore them every day.

I don't think I liked school. For one thing, learning wasn't fun like my first few grades in America. We didn't do any finger-painting, drawing turkeys, Christmas trees, and Santas. Nor did we play any games. From the very beginning, it was all reading, 'riting, and 'rithmetic. However, I still have one composition I wrote in the 2nd grade in which I described the wall and gates surrounding the little town of Lich where we moved to after our stay in Giessen-Wieseck. My first grade teacher was a one-legged war veteran who was very strict. He had a row of bamboo canes mounted on one wall which he used on any kids who misbehaved. I don't remember ever getting beaten. I think I was too scared of him to ever get into trouble.

Our grades ranged from a number 1 to 6 - one being excellent, and 6 a failing grade. I got mainly twos throughout my three years of grade school in Germany. Besides the three R's, there was also a grade for Beteiligung (deportment) for which I usually received a two.

One thing I did like doing from the time I learned to write, was drawing pictures. I almost always accompanied my written compositions and letters with drawings. My dad saved some of these for me. Once I learned how to write, I also loved writing letters to my dad and Elizabeth. But as much as I liked living in Giessen-Wieseck, my life was soon to change once again.

ONKEL JOSEF

You braved the Nazi terror by speaking out your truth,

You risked your very life and limb and sacrificed your youth,

Survived four years in Dachau in the belly of the beast,

Confronting death each day and night with your fellow priests.

I thank you, Onkel Josef, for what you did for me

You helped me get adopted, and set my spirit free.

You found a loving couple who faced down their own strife,

And took me from that orphanage to give a new life.

The gratitude I owe you will last a lifetime long,

You're in my thoughts and prayers and in this heartfelt song.

A trace of love and comfort you have left behind

For all those who have suffered in their hearts and minds,

You set a great example of what we all can be,

By following our better angels into eternity.

V – Summers in Poppenhausen

One thing that made the loss of my mom in 1951 less painful were my annual summer visits to Pfarrer Albinger and his housekeeper Rosa in Poppenhausen, a scenic mountain village near the East German border. Beginning in the summer after first grade, about six months after my mom's death, until I moved to the U.S.A. with my dad at the age of nine, I looked forward to these annual pilgrimages. Even though I was encouraged to call Pfarrer Albinger *Onkel* (Uncle) Josef, I was always a bit afraid of him since he was tall, austere looking, and had a somewhat intimidating presence. However, his housekeeper whom I called Tante Rosa, became like a second mom to me. She was very warm and affectionate and had a real way with children. In fact, while I stayed with them in their parish house, she was always surrounded by kids, and thrived on looking after them when their parents weren't available or otherwise indisposed.

During my stays in Poppenhausen, I was given a small upstairs room to sleep in. What I remember most about this room was the small wooden statue of the Christian martyr St. Sebastian that stood in one corner. It showed him impaled by half a dozen arrows which protruded from various parts of his body. Yet his face had an incongruously blissful look. Given my increasing fascination with Christ's passion as well as the often gory stories of the martyrs' deaths, that statue often gave me nightmares.

When I visited Onkel Josef and Tante Rosa 35 years later, I noticed that he had kept this statue which had now been moved to the front hallway. When I told Onkel Josef about my nightmares, he made an unforgettable gesture of being struck by an arrow. Then he told me that this statue had been carved by a famous German sculptor about 300 years ago.

The other thing I remembered about Onkel Josef was that the village church of which he was the *Dechant* (monsignor) was perennially under construction. There always seemed to be scaffolding around its outer walls. Besides this church, there was also a little chapel on top of a hill nearby. It was used as a storage place for various statues while the church was under construction. Along a pathway up the hill to the chapel, were the fourteen stations of the cross which I often visited. And on top of the hill next to the chapel was a giant-sized crucifix made of stone. Like the statue of St. Sebastian, I often fantasized about Christ's crucifixion, as well as the statues in the chapel which depicted Mary, the various disciples, and martyrs.

During those summers, I went to the village church every Sunday morning, usually with Tante Rosa, while Onkel Josef said mass. One time, I had an especially embarrassing moment that Tante Rosa thought was very funny and never let me forget. Getting dressed was always hard for me, especially after my mother's death. One Sunday morning, I woke up late for mass. So I rushed to get dressed. Since Tante Rosa was already in the church, I had to put on my clothes on my own. But I got it all wrong. I put on my jacket backwards, and put the wrong shoes on the wrong feet. Then I rushed into the church while mass was already in progress, ran down the center aisle in front of all the parishioners, looking frantically for Tante Rosa, who was sitting in front. When she saw me looking panicky and disheveled, she couldn't help but smile. Then she helped me straighten up my jacket, and put my shoes on right. But she never forgot this little incident which she would tell everyone.

Tante Rosa introduced me to some of the other kids who were visiting the parsonage. She or Onkel Josef often took us on *spaziergaenge* (hikes) to the two highest mountains in the nearby *Rhoengebirge* (Rhone Mountains). These were called *Kreuzberg* and *Die Wasserkuppe*. Die Wasserkuppe had been used during the 30s and 40s to train glider pilots. During one of these hikes, I was so awestruck by the mountain's grandeur that I exclaimed: "Wasserkuppe, du bist ein schoener berg!" (Wasserkuppe, you're a beautiful mountain!) On another one of these hikes, I accompanied a little girl named Christel who wore her hair in long pigtails, and a friend of hers. Tante Rosa took a picture of the three of us atop the mountain.

For reasons I have long since forgotten, I didn't always get along well with Christel who was about a year older than me. When I got angry about something she said to me, I would frequently pull her pigtails. Another time, we were both attending an evening Vespers service. I immediately ran over to Tante Rosa calling out loudly: "Wie kann ich Christel schlagen?" (How can I hit Christel?) After that, I didn't speak to Christel again.

During my stays, Onkel Josef would often teach me about the Catholic faith. He would tell me stories about Jesus, Mother Mary, the apostles, saints, and martyrs. Not only was I fascinated by these stories, but being a pious, scrupulous boy, I started fantasizing about them. I often imagined becoming a martyr myself. One time I asked Tante Rosa about something Onkel Josef had taught me. When she couldn't answer, I replied: *"Ich gehe lieber zu Onkel Josef. Er weiss bescheid!"* (I'd rather go to Uncle Josef. He knows the answer!).

Sometimes I got very judgmental about my faith. One time, after Onkel Josef had told me the story of Christ's passion and death, I told Tante Rosa that because the Jews had done such terrible things to Jesus, they should be punished. Shortly afterwards, I climbed up the hill on my way to the little chapel on top, looking for that station of the cross that showed where Jesus punished the Jews. When I couldn't find it, I was very disappointed.

During my visits in Poppenhausen in 1985 and 1989, Tante Rosa showed me a lots of pictures that she and Onkel Josef had taken of me and the other children they'd known, which she had carefully collected in various photo albums. These show me at ages six, seven, eight, and nine. During those times, I was very impressed by all the hard work she had to do. She not only cared for Onkel Josef, keeping his priestly vestments clean and pressed, but she also did all the cooking, cleaning, and tending to her garden, as well as looking after all the neighborhood kids who liked to hang around the parsonage. In fact, one time, feeling sorry for her, I told her: "Tante, Rosa, Du must zu viel arbeiten!" (Aunt Rosa, you've got to work too hard!). There was also one incident she told me about that gave me a valuable insight into my own scrupulous personality.

Tante Rosa had a big garden in front and back of the parsonage in which she grew all her own fruits and vegetables. There were peas, beans, lettuce, tomatoes, spinach, and carrots, as well as strawberries, raspberries, and gooseberries. There were also several fruit trees in the back yard like apple, pear, and plum trees. One summer, she asked me to pick some *steckrueben* (turnips) from her garden. But I forgot what she had told me and ended up picking *mohrrueben* (carrots) instead. When I got back to the house, proud of my achievement, eager to show what I had picked, she corrected me by telling me I'd picked the wrong vegetables. I got so upset with myself that I found a big stick and told her that Onkel Josef should punish me by giving me a beating. Tante Rosa just smiled and told me it was no big thing, just an understandable error, and that I certainly didn't deserve to be punished. When she told Onkel Josef, he also told me I certainly didn't deserve to be punished for something so trivial.

Starting around the time of my first Communion and reinforced by my my religious instruction by Onkel Josef, I became increasingly devout. I think the strong feelings I had for Jesus, Mary, and the saints were a substitute in some way, for the feelings of grief over the loss of my mother, that I didn't know how to deal with since my dad didn't talk about her after she died. Although I missed her a lot, especially after returning home from my summer visits, I didn't know how to express those feelings.

During Holy Week, I began to fantasize about suffering like Jesus, taking part in his Passion and death on the cross. I even imagined fashioning myself a crown of thorns, constructing a cross from two pieces of wood, and carrying it up a hill on Good Friday. Every year before Easter Sunday, I looked forward to doing the stations of the cross. My religious fantasies continued as I grew older, but I never dared reveal them to anyone. It was own my little secret that I guarded closely because I felt that grownups wouldn't understand, and that I might be punished if I told them to anyone.

This fear was reinforced after I read the story of the three little Portugese girls in Fatima, who witnessed a vision of the Virgin Mary in a hillside grotto. I really identified with them. They not only claimed that they had seen the Virgin Mary appear to them several times, but they also witnessed another miracle – the sun spinning around itself. But when they told their parish priest about their visions, they were not only not believed,but also punished, and ordered to recant. They were told these visions weren't real. They were just figments of their imagination, probably prompted by the devil. I was scared something similar would happen to me if I ever revealed my own religious fantasies to anyone.

I continued to look forward to these annual visits to Poppenhausen until I was nine years old and ready to come to the U.S. I always looked forward to seeing Tante Rosa and Onkel Josef, eating their wonderful meals, and meeting some of the kids that visited the parsonage. I think that Tante Rosa's love and caring sustained me throughout the frequent moves I was forced to make. My Poppenhausen visits gave me a stable base that I could count on.

FIRST FRIENDS

First friends, first friends
Are the first ones you met,
First friends, first friends
You will never forget.
Through hard times and lean,
They'll stay by your side,
Through tough times and mean,
They'll be your true guides.

VI – First Friends in Lich

By now, moving had become a regular ritual for me and my dad. Just before I started second grade when I was seven years old, my dad had to move again because the military government was transferring him to yet another safe house, this time in a little town near Giessen-Wieseck called Lich. This new house seemed like palace, more like a mansion than an ordinary home. I don't remember much about the rooms inside the house except they were many and large compared to what I had been used to. I even had my own bedroom. There were also two bathrooms, one on each floor, something I'd never seen before.

But what impressed me most was the huge garden in back with its many trees and bushes. Also, all along the rear of the house was a long wooden trellis covered with vines. I still have a photo of it at night when my dad strung it with many brightly colored paper lanterns for one very memorable *Fasching* (Carnival) party he held in February 1952.

He invited a lot of people, most of whom he'd gotten to know through work, including a general and his wife. There was also Dr. Mutschmann and his wife, Pfarrer Albinger, our housekeeper Elizabeth, Frau Euler, and her son Arnold. My dad had painted an elaborate Japanese-style landscape for the occasion which depicted a crooked, ornate tree. It was hung on one living room wall. His guests were all invited to come in costume. I remember that my dad was dressed as The Mad Hatter out of *Alice in Wonderland*. One of the other guests came dressed as a pirate.

My dad dressed me up with two pieces of white cardboard hung from my shoulders on my front and back, painted with two red hearts, depicting the Two of Hearts from *Alice in Wonderland*. I was also given a small bucket and a paint brush with which I was supposed to paint the white roses red. My job was to make a brief appearance in front of the adults at the beginning of the party before I had to go to bed. I didn't like having to wear a costume, but it was exciting to be allowed to mingle with the grownups, albeit briefly. But I didn't get much out of all their talking which I found boring. I was just sorry there were no other kids to play with.

One thing that made adjusting to my new home in Lich much easier for me was the fact that our housekeeper from Giessen-Wieseck, Elizabeth, continued working for my dad by doing the cooking, cleaning, and taking care of me after school, until my dad got home from work. She had to take the train each weekday from Giessen-Wieseck to get there. She was like a second mom to me, and made losing my own mom less painful. Besides Tante Rosa in Poppenhausen, she was definitely one of my favorite people. In fact, some of the kids I played with thought she was my mom, as was the case in Giessen-Wieseck. In the spring of 1952, I started attending second grade at a new school. Although I don't remember anything about my classes, I do recall that my new teacher was another man. However, he wasn't the stern disciplinarian I'd had in first grade. For one thing, there were no canes in his classroom.

In the summer and fall of 1952, there were two big events that changed my life. One was celebrating my first Communion and the other was making my first new friends.

My first Communion turned out to be a big celebration. During mass, I was given a tall, white, ornate candle to mark the occasion. I was told I could light it on special holydays. I remember I had to dress up in a formal pair of black shorts and a white shirt. After mass, I carried my lit candle in a big procession through the streets of town. When the procession ended, my dad held another one of his big parties to which he invited all his friends like Dr.Mutschmann and his wife, Onkel Josef from Poppenhausen, Elizabeth, and many others. For a brief moment I basked in all their attention.

A few weeks later I had a chance to march in another procession, this time to celebrate *Fronleichnam* (Corpus Christi) in the month of June. I was given a large banner, but had a devil of a time holding it upright.

My embarrassing moment was preserved forever by a photo my dad took of me with his new Voigtländer camera. In fact, he gave me an entire photo album depicting scenes from my first Communion and the Fronleichnam parade.

But by far the biggest event of my seventh year was making my first friends: Adolf Maruschka and Walter Kreuzinger. I met them both at school, and, although they were a few years older than me, they took me under their wing. They provided me with the steady companionship I had lacked until then. They both loved nature, especially that favorite German activity *spazierengehen* (hiking outdoors). The three of us took lots of walks together, especially on weekends. They taught me how to climb trees. And since they were both altar boys, they taught me how to serve mass. While they alternated in taking on the role of priest, I became their acolyte. One of their moms, who was very religious, sewed them priest-like vestments, and made them a white altar cloth. We put white candles on a table that served as an altar. We used glasses of water and apple juice to simulate the priest's water and wine. Playing mass became one of my favorite activities since I was becoming increasingly pious after my first Communion. As in Poppenhausen, I was I was fascinated by the lives of the saints and martyrs. I not only identified strongly with Christ's sufferings on the cross, but looked forward to doing the stations of the cross at church. I still had those fantasies of fashioning my own wooden cross to carry on Good Friday.

Many years later, in 1989, during one of my visits back in Germany, I had a chance to be re-united with both Adolf and Walter. To my amazement, they both still lived in the same little town where I had known them when I was seven. Both of them were now married, had children of their own, and worked as grade school teachers. Seeing them again after more than 35 years felt no short of miraculous. We shared old memories like playing priest and altar boy at mass. They also remembered that I always looked unkempt and disheveled in school, like a little boy that didn't have a mother to set him straight and teach him how to dress. Adolf also developed a close bond with my dad whom he'd visit regularly in our mansion of a house. They would have long, nightly discussions in which they talked about everything under the sun from politics, to music, to literature. My dad became a mentor to him.

In Lich, my favorite time of year was Christmas. My dad didn't get a Christmas tree until about a week before the holiday. He placed it in the large living room, set it upright in a metal holder under which he placed a pan filled with water. But I wasn't allowed to see it until the evening of the 24th. Then he let me into the living room to see the tree for the first time. It was decorated with red beeswax candles that were secured to the branches with metal holders. It was covered with strands of silver *lametta* (tinsel). On top, my dad had placed a silver star. And of course what I was most excited about where the piles of many-colored presents stacked on a little table beneath the tree. I couldn't wait to see what I would get this year.

I don't remember if we had celebrated Christmas the year before since my mom was in the hospital at the time. That made this year all the more special. But as much as I wanted to open the presents immediately, my dad had other ideas. First, there were some important rituals to observe. I think he really enjoyed prolonging the suspense of making me wait for gifts to be opened. He began the festivities by slowly and carefully lighting the candles on the tree, starting from the top and proceeding to the bottom. Then Elizabeth served us some cups of hot chocolate. Afterwards, he led us all in singing Christmas carols like *Ihr Kinderlein Kommet* (O Come all Ye Children), *O Du Froehliche* (O Ye Happy Ones), *Kling, Gloeckchen Kling* (Ring Little Bells Ring), and of course *Stille Nacht* (Silent Night).

By now I could hardly contain my excitement. So, when my dad finally gave the signal, I lit into my presents like a wild man, tearing open the wrapping paper to see what treasures lay inside. I don't recall what gifts I got that year except for one. It was elaborately wrapped in a large box. My dad told me to be careful when I opened it. Inside was an HO-gauge miniature model train. Not only did it have a bright shining black locomotive with several dark green interlocking train cars that were individually wrapped in crepe paper, but there were also many lengths of straight and curved stainless tracks that could be linked together. The black locomotive with its tiny green cars looked like miniature versions of the real trains I had seen. There was also a little train station with tiny light bulbs that made it glow in the dark. There were papier-mâché hills and tunnels for the train could go up and through. There were also little houses and other buildings that could be lit with the tiny light bulbs set inside them.

At first, I was so overwhelmed by this expensive gift, that I didn't know what to do. I was almost too scared to touch it for fear of breaking something, and making my dad angry. I was also a bit disappointed since I'd been hoping for a toy that didn't take so much time assembling, and that I could play with right away like a spinning top, a set of marbles, or a board game like *Mensch ärgere Dich nicht!* which is similar to Sorry.

But my dad was in seventh heaven as if he'd just gotten the gift. Without waiting for me, he immediately started linking the tracks together by its couplings until he formed a large loop of tracks on the floor. Then he unwrapped the rest of the green cars, hooked them up to the locomotive, and set them on the tracks. He told me to be careful as he hooked up the electrical cord to power the train and plugged it into the nearest socket. He let me turn on the switch so I could watch the train run around its track. He was like a ten year old boy who had just gotten his favorite gift. He spent the rest of that evening, all day Christmas, and the next week assembling that entire train set and its surroundings, painting and decorating the paper-mache hills and tunnels, setting up the miniature train station and houses that he placed carefully beside the tracks. While he busied himself with this task, I grew increasingly bored, and soon turned to some of the other toys I'd gotten. I think my dad was a bit disappointed that I wasn't more enthusiastic about this expensive new gift.

I think that my two-year stay in Lich was the happiest time I'd experienced yet, what with the beautiful, mansion-like house we lived in, my first Communion, my two new friends, and all those parties my dad hosted. I was also happy that Elizabeth continued taking care of me. But that was all to change too soon as my dad was transferred to yet another safe house. This one was located in a large city South of Marburg called Giessen.

VII – A Sad Farewell in Giessen

The toughest time of my childhood, besides my eighteen months in the orphanage and the period just after my mother's death, was my final year in Germany, just before coming to the U.S. with my dad in October 1954. Like many times before, my dad had to move again to another safe house, this time in a larger city named Giessen, located about 50 kilometers South of Marburg. I had to start third grade at yet another school. But I don't remember anything about it except that I was very lonely and unhappy there. I didn't make any new friends. Nor do I recall if my dad hired another housekeeper to replace Elizabeth who had left to get married. I probably had to take care of myself after school until my dad came home from work to fix dinner.

I really missed my old friends Adolf and Walter in Lich, not to mention Tante Rosa and Onkel Josef in Poppenhausen. Besides attending school, I spent most of the time by myself except for weekends when I could be with my dad to take long walks or play games. The house we lived in was a large stucco house on the corner of a street in the center of Giessen. I remember nothing of its interior. But it had a large back yard overgrown with bushes and trees. It was surrounded by an iron fence on all sides. That was symbolic of the way I felt then – fenced in and alone.

I have hardly any memories of my stay in Giessen except for one vague one. I think I went to a soup kitchen regularly to have lunch, or it may have been an evening meal, I don't remember which. I remember being served a thick split pea soup, something I like to this day.

Although my mom and dad had originally planned to emigrate to the U.S. long before 1954, circumstances got in the way. After my mom contracted cancer in 1950, any plans to come to the U.S. had to be put on hold because my dad had to spend what little money he had saved on her expensive, yet ineffective treatments. By the time my mom died in January of 1951, his savings had been used up. Fortunately, his dreams of coming to America were resurrected about three years later.

Besides translating for the Americans, my dad also earned some extra money by tutoring several GIs he'd met through work. One of them was named Jim Ahlrichs. One day Jim asked him if he had ever thought about emigrating to America. When my dad objected because he had no sponsor in the U.S. to vouch for him, Jim offered to ask his dad in Cincinnati, Ohio to become his sponsor. Thus my dad's dream of emigrating was renewed. This time fate smiled upon him. Because he had been working for the Americans, had saved up enough money, and now had someone to sponsor him, he could definitely plan such a trip. Jim assured him that he could live in his dad's home in Cincinnati until he found a job and a place to live. However, things did not turn out as well as Jim had predicted.

Finally, in early October 1954, my dad was ready to embark on our long journey to America. We first had to get our passport photos taken. I still have them in one of my photo albums. Then we said goodbye to all our friends, including Tante Lucie and her daughter Ali whom I hadn't seen in years. We then took the train to Bremen in the north of Germany. We spent a day touring the city. I remember that my dad took a picture of me standing next to a giant statue of Roland , the medieval German hero who was celebrated in a famous epic poem. The statue stood in the large, ornate, market square. Then we had to take another train to Bremerhaven, the large harbor on the outskirts of Bremen from which transatlantic ships began their voyages, many of them to America.

I felt a mixture of excitement and fear. I really missed all the people I'd gotten to know in Wershausen, Marburg, Poppenhausen, Giessen-Wieseck, and Lich, especially my friends Adolf and Walter, as well as our housekeeper Elizabeth, Tante Lucie, Ali, Tante Rosa and Onkel Josef. But I was also very excited about crossing the vast Atlantic ocean on an ocean liner, bound for a new land that I could not imagine. Yes, I was about to embark on the biggest journey of my life.

Sometimes, when I think back on my year in Giessen, I wonder why I can't remember more of that time. I think it has a lot to do with the fact that I felt very lonely there, missed my old friends, and didn't like my new school. I also missed Elizabeth who no longer worked for my dad because she had gotten married. Also, there were few photos from that time that could have jogged my memory. To me, it was just another of many moves, this time to a large and impersonal city. The one thing I do remember about Giessen was all the construction that was being done in the city to repair or rebuild the bombed out buildings. I loved playing in some of the bomb craters, as well as the ruined buildings. For example, I remember seeing one building whose entire side had been blown away, exposing its interior. In one corner of the house was a fully intact bathtub.

I often wish that I could remember more of what I experienced growing up in Germany until the age of nine. But I'm very glad I was able to collect the stories I did from my dad, Tante Lucie, Onkel Josef, Tante Rosa, Walter and Adolf, and the other people I got to know growing up, and whom I revisited as an adult.

PART II
Growing Up in America

LET THE OCEAN TAKE ME HOME

It was many, many years ago when I first came to these shores
With my father on a great big ship because he was seeking more,
We steamed into New York Harbor past the Statue of Liberty,
A little foreign boy of nine, didn't know what my future'd be.
Let the ocean take me home where I need no longer roam,
Where the waves roll high and the seagulls fly
Let the ocean take me home.
Let the ocean take me home where the swells the dry sands comb,
Where the clouds sweep by 'neath a clear blue sky,
Let the ocean take me home.
Well, I learned the English language, went to school
in my new home town,
Became a U. S. citizen, got a job, and settled down,
But sometimes when my heart is low, my thoughts drift overseas
To my German friends and family in a land I cannot see.
I've been wandering all my life down these many roads,
Looking for a place to rest and restore my soul,
I've felt lots of joy and pain, faced a lot of fears,
Up and down this rollercoaster ride of seventy years.

I – A Storm in Mid-Crossing

It all started about a week into our ocean crossing. My dad and I had embarked upon a two-and-a-half-week voyage from Bremerhaven, West Germany to America aboard an old, creaky, Greek ocean liner on its last legs called The Neptunia. It had only one funnel and wasn't that impressive as ocean liners go, but for me, a nine-year-old boy, it was the adventure of a lifetime.

Shortly before noon, about seven days out, the wind started blowing and howling, the waves got higher and higher. In the large dining room where we ate our meals, the ship's crew had secured everything that wasn't fastened down to prevent the passengers from being injured by flying debris. They had also sprayed the white linen tablecloths with water.

I had just made my way to my favorite part of the ship to watch the waves crashing against its prow, and to marvel at the white, sudsy foam which crested the waves. I felt the cold sea spray on my face, smelled the sea air mixed with diesel fumes, and tasted the salty water on my lips. As the wind blew stronger, I could see the mast ropes swinging to and fro, and the ship's Greek flag flapping wildly atop the mast like an angry bird. I watched the ship's prow plunge down into the crashing waves, then rise again to meet the next wave again and again. I had to hold onto the ship's railing to keep myself from falling over. I observed some crew members in their starched white uniforms guiding the few remaining passengers on deck back inside the ship.

My dad came up to me and told me we needed to head inside to be safe. We walked along several narrow corridors to get to our tiny second class stateroom on one of the lower decks. There my dad asked me to take a small white pill. After I swallowed mine, he also took one.

"Tony, this is the Dramamine tablet I told you about that prevents sea-sickness. Remember how we started taking them a few days before our voyage, so our bodies could adjust, and we wouldn't get sick once we were on the ship? I overheard someone say that this was going to be quite a storm, so I want us to be prepared."

It was time for lunch, so we headed to the second-class dining room a deck above our stateroom. It was a large room with a very low ceiling and lots of round tables bedecked with white table cloths. I saw a few waiters standing around, but there was hardly anyone there but us. As if reading my mind, my dad explained, "You know, Tony, you can see we're practically the only ones here. I bet the others are all sea-sick. They probably didn't have the foresight to take those pills. How are you feeling? You're not getting sick, are you?

I told him I wasn't sea-sick, but I wasn't hungry either. "But you need to eat something to keep up your strength. I think you should at least have some soup."

I didn't want to get into an argument with my dad, so I went along. When a waiter finally came to our table, my dad ordered a sandwich and salad for himself and soup for me. While waiting for our food to arrive, I noticed that the white table cloths had all been wetted down with water.

"Papa, why did they wet down the table cloths?"

"Can't you guess? It's so they won't slide off the tables during the storm."

After our waiter came with our food, the ship was rocking up and down so much, I had a hard time spooning the soup into my mouth without spilling half of it onto the floor. My dad too struggled with his salad. Suddenly, the whole situation struck me as utterly absurd, so I started laughing hysterically.

"What's so funny, Tony?"

I didn't know what to say, but I found the whole scene to be ridiculously funny. Here we were, the two of us, practically alone in the dining room trying to eat while the other passengers were probably throwing up in their staterooms as the ship swayed from side to side. My dad too caught the absurdity of the situation. And we both had ourselves a good laugh.

"Well, Tony, I guess we've both gotten ourselves more of an adventure than we'd bargained for!"

II – Who's the Leader of the Band?

When my dad and I emigrated from Germany to the U.S when I was nine in October 1954, he had a hard time getting established in the new country. For one thing, we had no relatives to help us, only his sponsoring family who lived in Cincinnati, Ohio. One of my dad's colleagues in Germany, Jim Ahlrichs, had encouraged him to emigrate so he could get his degree, something he could not have done in Germany because he didn't have the financial resources.

My first memories of being in the new country were positive ones.

We moved in with the Ahlrichs in a wealthy suburb of Cincinnati called Price Hill. Although I had completed the 3rd grade in Germany, my dad had me start the 3rd grade over again since I didn't speak a word of English. He told me later that I learned the new language quickly and was fairly fluent after only six months.

I don't remember much about my new school except for the fact that it was a Catholic parochial school and seemed like a party after the rigors of my German classroom. My new teacher was a sympathetic young woman who made me feel welcome and made learning fun. She had us do lots of enjoyable things like finger painting. Before Thanksgiving, she passed out crayons and had us draw pictures of turkeys. She also passed out red, blue, silver, and gold stars when we did well in our homework. I really liked all the art projects and remember drawing lots of pictures of ocean liners since my memories of my Atlantic crossing were still fresh in my mind.

My first Christmas in America was both overwhelming and unforgettable, quite a contrast from the more modest Christmas Eve celebrations I had experienced in Germany. Here we had an enormous Christmas tree with lots of colored lights, tinsel, and numerous presents piled underneath it. The radio played non-stop, popular Christmas songs I'd never heard of before like *Jingle Bells*, *Rudolf the Red-Nosed Reindeer*, and *Santa Claus is Coming to Town*.

Another positive memory of that first year in America was my visit with Kvet, a woman my dad dated briefly. He had gotten to know her in Germany, and she met us in New York City where she took us to the Empire State Building. I remember being awestruck by my view of the huge city from on top of that skyscraper. Kvet and her teenage daughter now lived in Maryland where she invited us to stay one weekend in their new apartment. I can still recall how much I liked the sugar-coated Honey Crisp cereal she served me for breakfast. It was a real treat for me since my dad never let me eat sweetened cereals because he deemed them unhealthy. Unfortunately, we didn't visit Kvet again because my dad felt she was pressuring him to get married. For another thing, their values didn't match up well. She wanted a husband who earned a lot of money, whereas my dad knew that he would never earn a big salary if he succeeded in his dream of becoming a college professor. Added to that, he believed that Kvet was spoiling her daughter.

In spite of these positive first impressions, my excitement and joy at living in the new country was short-lived. What my dad couldn't have known is that Jim's father was very unsympathetic towards Germans even though his family had originally come from Germany. Not only did he not allow German to be spoken in his home, but he pressured my dad to move out as soon as possible.

Fortunately, my dad was already fluent in English, so he soon got a full-time position as file-clerk for The Southern Railroad. But this new position proved so taxing physically that by the end of each week, he felt totally exhausted. On top of that, he spent most of his weekday evenings and Saturday mornings attending classes at Xavier University so he could get his Masters degree in English Literature and start teaching there.

All that left him little time to take care of me, a nine-year old boy whose mother had died four years before, and who didn't know a word of English. He tried to cope with this untenable situation by renting a cheap small room, provided by the railroad, in downtown Cincinnati, while placing me in a foster home he had found out about through Catholic Charities. This home was located in Fort Thomas, Kentucky, a small town across the Ohio River from Cincinnati. I stayed there during the spring and summer of 1955 when I was ten. I remember next to nothing about my stay, only what my dad told me.

He said, for example, that my foster mom would make me sit on the floor of her living room after I'd returned from school, rolling back the carpet, so I wouldn't ruin it. She wouldn't even allow me to sit on the couch or armchairs. I would spend the entire time alone watching T.V. This did have the one positive effect speeding up my process of learning English. But my dad could sense I was very unhappy there in the hands of this incompetent and neglectful caretaker. He finally arranged through Catholic Charities to find me another home.

At first, this second home seemed a step up because it was located in a large, old, ramshackle house in a small, bucolic town about fifty miles from Cincinnati called Blanchester. The house had a large backyard with lots of trees and a rabbit hutch. We often had rabbit stew for dinner. The foster family had about a dozen boys aged 8 to 12 years old.

However, I was even more unhappy in the Blanchester house than I had been in Forth Thomas. I don't remember anyone making feel welcome. Plus I had to start another new school. One of the few positive things I can recall were my dad's weekly visits on Sunday afternoons. The other was watching TV in the basement. On Sunday nights they always showed *Walt Disney Presents*. Disney's magical worlds of Adventurel Land, Frontier Land, Fantasyland, and Tomorrow Land captured my imagination, temporarily relieving my intense loneliness. I also remember playing marbles and collecting rocks on my way home from school.

When my dad saw how unhappy I was in Blanchester, he feared for the worst, and was concerned about my becoming more and more withdrawn and uncommunicative. Fortunately, an unexpected benefactor came to our rescue. One of my dad's professors at Xavier University, Dr. Paul Harkins, offered to let me move in with his large Catholic family of eight.

So, in the winter of 1956 I moved in with The Harkins. The contrast from Blanchester couldn't have been greater. The one downside was that I had to start yet another school, but this time I was welcomed into my new family. The Harkins were a loving yet chaotic family. The mother ruled her brood of eight with a frenetic pace worthy of The Energizer Bunnny.

Their youngest girl was a baby nicknamed Quinky, so named because she was born on Quinquagesima Sunday (the Sunday before Lent), who banged her spoon in her high chair, demanding to be fed. The two teenage girls spent all evening talking with their boyfriends on the phone, or listening to Elvis and Pat Boone records.

In the meantime their mother Rhea did all she could to keep up with her kids, washing and drying endless loads of laundry, cooking meals, and cleaning up after her kids. Their dad, Dr. Harkins, spent most of his time in his upstairs study grading student papers, preparing tests, and working on his research projects. At the time of my stay, he was working on a book about St. John Chrisostom.

The oldest boy, Patrick, who was about a year older than me, quickly took me under his wing and introduced me to his school friends. He showed me how to play baseball and often took me along on his paper route after school. I can still remember going to those big, old, musty-smelling brown-brick apartment buildings to help him with his deliveries.

Patrick was not only generous but also very inventive. One of my favorite memories was when he showed me how to make a primitive telephone by connecting two coffee cans with a string that he tightened between them. While he would talk into the can on one end, I'd listen to him on the other.

I also loved watching TV with the younger kids. My favorite shows were westerns like *Hop-along-Cassidy* and *The Lone Ranger*, as well as *The Mickey Mouse Club*. I can still hear that refrain: "Who's the leader of the band that's made for you and me? —M-I-C— See you real soon —K-E-Y— Why? Because we like you! M-O-U-S-E."

I also fell in love with a new animated Disney film called *Fantasia* which featured well-known classical compositions such as *The Nutcracker Suite* and the *Sorcerer's Apprentice* . It made a huge musical impression on me.

During that winter a new made-for-TV-movie hit the airwaves that both kids and adults went crazy for: *Davy Crockett, King of the Wild Frontier*. I eagerly followed the exploits of the frontiersman who "Killed him a 'bar' when he was only three." Like almost every other American boy from six to twelve, I wanted a coonskin cap, a little a little plastic horn with fake gun powder, and a replica of the flint-lock rifle that Crockett used. I also acquired a cap gun with a holster, and learned to play cowboys and Indians with the Harkins boys and the other kids in the neighborhood.

In the summer of 1956, my dad finally moved into his own apartment about a mile and a half from the Harkins. I remember visiting him Sunday afternoons, walking up that endless hill on Clifton Avenue to his new apartment in Volkert Place. He would often prepare me a treat of home-made ice cream, which he made by freezing chocolate milk into ice cube trays.

At the end of that summer, my dad arranged to have me to move back in with him. This would mean having to start yet another school. As much as I had enjoyed my Sunday afternoon visits with my dad, I didn't really want to leave the Harkins, say goodbye to my friend Patrick, and live as an only child again. But the decision wasn't mine to make, and I didn't know how to express my true feelings to my dad. After all, I had learned that *Father Knows Best*.

So in the fall of 1956, I moved back with my dad, started fifth grade at St. Monica's parochial school, said goodbye forever to my life with the Harkins and foster care. I was about to embark on another chapter in my life.

III – Fossils and the Friar's Club

Leaving the Harkins family in the fall of 1956 was very difficult for me. Even though I should have been glad to be reunited with my dad after living in three foster homes, the transition turned out to be a painful one. For one thing, I had to start fifth grade in yet another school, St. Monica's. For another, I missed Pat Harkins, and didn't want to be alone again.

My father's new apartment in Volkert Place was located in the Clifton neighborhood of Cincinnati, not far from the University of Cincinnati, where he was starting to take graduate classes and work on his PhD. It was situated next to a small a hill which I often climbed. There I found lots of fossils in the limestone deposits. I had already started collecting rocks in Blanchester, but I found fossils more interesting because of their link to dinosaurs.

But I had a hard time making friends at St. Monica's. I ended up spending most of my time alone, collecting rocks, reading, or listening to my dad's growing classical music collection. With the little money he was able to save on his meager instructor's salary, he had started to amass an extensive collection of classical long-playing records, including the symphonies of Beethoven, Brahms, Tchaikovsky, and Dvorak, as well as the operas of Wagner, Verdi, and Puccini. One of his other records that made a big impression on me was Sergei Prokoffiev's tone poem *Peter and the Wolf*. My father explained to me that this piece was based on a Russian folk tale whose characters were introduced by their own distinctive musical leit-motifs, played by the different instruments in the orchestra like the oboe, bassoon, and French horn. I was very intrigued and soon imagined myself becoming a composer of classical music like Prokoffiev or Beethoven.

Around this time I also developed an interest in poetry, thanks to the encouragement of my fifth grade teacher, a kindly and understanding nun. My first poems were rhyming odes dedicated to the mailman and milkman. Unfortunately, I've lost them all.

In 1957, my dad helped his best friend from Germany, Arnold Euler, immigrate to the U.S. Arnold moved in and stayed with us for about nine months until he was able to find a place of his own. Although Arnold worked as a printer, his real passion was music. He had a beautiful tenor voice, loved opera like my dad, and began taking voice lessons at the nearby Cincinnati Conservatory of Music. I can still remember him practicing arias from Verdi's *Rigoletto* or Puccinis *La Boheme*. Not only could he sing, but he was also very handsome, charming, and outgoing, everything I was not. I began to look up to him like an older brother.

Arnold supplemented my dad's classical music collection with his own recordings of famous tenors like Mario Lanzo, John McCormick, and his favorite, Enrico Caruso. He and my dad often joined forces in singing arias from *Madame Butterfly*, *Tosca* and *Turandot*. I often heard them fantasize about him becoming the next renowned tenor and singing sensation from Germany: Arnoldo Wiesecko! I too loved listening to Arnold's Caruso records even though I never wanted to become an opera singer. It was enough for me to bask in Arnold's reflected glory.

So, when Arnold moved out of my dad's apartment in 1958, I really missed him. I didn't like being alone again with my dad. Transitioning into sixth grade also proved difficult. For one thing, my sixth grade teacher wasn't as supportive as my fifth grade teacher had been. She was more of a disciplinarian who didn't encourage my creativity. I gradually stopped writing poems. I still wasn't able to make any new friends in my new grade, spending most of my time alone.

This caused my dad to be concerned enough to devise some ways to get me out of the house. His first idea was a great one. He bought me a beautiful, brand new, three-speed Schwinn bicycle. I loved the bike immediately, but had some problems learning to ride it. Nor was my dad the most patient of teachers. But after lots of trial and error, several falls, and a bruised ego, I finally learned to keep myself balanced on two wheels. Once I got the hang of it, I rode my new bike everywhere I could. But one problem remained. Riding my bike was a solitary activity that didn't induce me to make new friends. So, my dad came up with another plan that he hoped would not only help me meet other boys my age, but would also build up my physical strength.

At that time I was thin and scrawny with stick-like arms and little upper body strength. So my dad signed me up for a weekly swimming program at a YMCA-like health club for kids and adults called The Friar's Club. It was located about a mile and a half from my apartment. I started going there every Saturday morning for a couple of hours. Since my dad didn't have a car yet, and there was no bus connection, I had to either walk or ride my bike.

At first I was excited at the prospect of swimming regularly because I'd always loved the water and hadn't had a chance to swim since I lived at the Harkins. But what I couldn't have anticipated was the teasing I'd have to deal with at the hands of the other boys who went there every Saturday morning. They didn't bother me in the pool because there were adults around. But the locker room was another matter. The worst part was having to undress to get into my swimming trunks. I was extremely self-conscious about my scrawny body and skinny arms and legs. As much as I would try to hurry up my changing into swimming trunks so the other boys wouldn't notice me, it didn't work. I often heard them snicker and poke fun at me behind my back. Sometimes they'd flick the wetted ends of their towels at me. I was always terrified that one day a group of boys would gang up on me after I left the locker room and beat me up. Fortunately, that never happened, but the fear never left me. Even though I enjoyed my time in the water, I hated going to The Friar's Club every week.

When I finally got up the nerve to tell my dad about my fears, he told me that I needed to face up to the bullies and not run away. So, the weekly visits continued, leaving me alone with my fears. Fortunately, I was never beaten up, but I lost some self-respect along the way because I never stood up to the boys that taunted me.

IV – 1457 Dana

My thirteenth year was the most tumultuous and difficult of my life since immigrating to the U.S. It was a year full of many big changes and shifts. Not only was I starting to feel the onset of puberty, but there was also another major move and another new school.

My dad's friend Arnold moved out of our Volkert Place apartment in 1958 in order to return to Germany to marry his childhood sweetheart Hannelore. When he returned to the U.S., he and Hannelore moved into their own apartment. By this time, my dad was earning enough as a college teacher to buy his first home. The house he bought was located close to Xavier University where he was now employed as a full-time instructor in English literature. He was also working on his PhD at The University of Cincinnati.

We moved into our new 1457 Dana Avenue home in the Evanston-Avondale neighborhood of Cincinnnati in the spring of 1958. It was a modest, one story stucco house located on a sharp curve in the road, just across from the Xavier campus. Our new home had a small front yard facing the street, a fenced in back yard, and a small one-car garage built into the basement of the house. It would be my home for the next eight years until I moved into a dorm on the Xavier campus.

This move was hard enough in itself, but even harder for me was having to start yet another school – my fifth since coming to the U.S. Since my dad was determined on my getting a first-class education, he enrolled me in an academically superior college prep junior high school called Walnut Hills where I started the 7th grade in the fall of 1958. This meant that I had to walk about two miles to get to my new school. It was a difficult adjustment since it had been only a fifteen minute walk to get to St. Monica's from my Volkert Place apartment. Of course the new neighborhood was totally unfamiliar to me and that made it even scarier.

Attending junior high was a harrowing experience for me. Everything was different than I had been used to in grade school. Instead of having one teacher for all my classes, I now had to get used to a different teacher for every subject. The only consistent teacher was my home room teacher. I stayed with the same kids for all my classes. I did not feel as safe and protected as I had in parochial school. Everything felt more rushed and impersonal. And the subjects were a lot harder. I started taking challenging classes like Latin, Algebra, Gym, and Shop. I'd often spend two or three hours a night doing homework.

But the classes and homework weren't the hardest thing about junior high. It was dealing with my new classmates. Although 7th grade went fairly well, and I got very good grades in most of my classes, by the time I got to the 8th grade, things took a turn for the worse. I recall being scared to go to school each morning for fear of being teased and bullied because I was so different and didn't fit in with the other kids. I was also quite a loner, and didn't know how to make friends. Even though I never got into any physical fights, I was often taunted verbally. Nor did it help that I was from Germany since World World War II and the Holocaust were still fresh in people's minds. I don't recall if the kids called me any names, but I do remember one boy named Jeffrey Rosen who gave me an especially hard time. Probably the fact that he was Jewish and I was German didn't help.

I remember especially dreading gym because I was so skinny and unathletic. Plus I hadn't played any sports except those pick-up baseball games with Patrick Harkins while living with his family in foster care. Thus I was always the last one chosen for any kinds of games and physical contests.

Since this was junior high, and everyone was dealing with puberty, the kids used a lot of raunchy humor. The magazine the boys liked the best was *Mad* with its cover depicting the nerdy looking Alfred E. Newman whose catchphrase was, "What, me worry?" The boys also loved reading comic books like Superman and Batman. I knew nothing about any of these. Nor was I familiar with all the new TV shows the kids were watching since my dad hadn't bought a TV yet. So that made me all the more vulnerable to being teased about my ignorance of pop culture.

The stress I was under, especially during the 8th grade, took a physical toll on me. Since I didn't play sports or had any physical outlet except gym class and that long walk to and from school, I developed a number of nervous ticks and twitches which just gave the kids more things to pick on. My father really became concerned when I developed a bad case of psoriasis on my elbows and knees. To remedy the situation, he took me to see a dermatologist who prescribed a foul-smelling, tar-like ointment, as well as regular sun lamp treatments. So, for the next few years, I would have to lie down on my basement bed for twenty minutes two or three times a week.

One of the few positive memories I have in junior high happened when I was in the 7th grade. I remember liking my English teacher – Helen Gerwig. She encouraged me to write stories. I remember getting an A in a story I wrote entitled *A Gift for Sid* which was inspired by Mark Twain's *Tom Sawyer*, a book I fell in love with. I still have this story. Another positive memory was reading Homer's *Odyssey* which contained stories we liked to reenact.

The happiest memory of Junior High, however, was joining the Walnut Hills Junior High School Band. I was given a flute and learned to play it so I could join the band. We'd play for football games and performed for school concerts. It was a real thrill to discover that I had a talent for music. It also gave me an outlet for expressing my pent-up emotions. But even here my joy was tainted. I still remember one of the band kids putting chewing gum on my chair, so that when I sat down, I had a wad of gum stuck to my rear end.

While attending junior high, I remember more of what I did outside of school, than what happened in school. One of the things I looked forward to was starting piano lessons at the age of fourteen with our church organist Helen Gough. My dad had purchased an old upright piano that had once been a player piano. So, every Saturday morning I would take a half hour walk to get to Miss Gough's home for my hour-long lesson. Although I enjoyed learning to play pieces like Beethoven's *Moonlight Sonata*, Mozart's *Turkish Rondo*, Satie's *Gymnopedia*, and Debussy's *Claire de Lune*, I didn't like having to play scales and those endless, boring Clementi exercises. I'd often put off practicing until the last minute which only infuriated my dad. Eventually, things came to a head and my dad got rid of the piano.

Another thing I looked forward to was visiting my dad's German friends Hannelore and Arnold in their new apartment, which was located near some beautiful woods. Hannelore prepared sumptious German meals while Arnold and my dad talked shop and teased each other about their respective jobs. Arnold claimed that my dad had it made because he got paid for talking. And my dad teased Arnold about the fact that, as a printer, all he had to do was push some buttons to operate the presses. Sometimes Arnold would bring out his violin, or my dad and he would sing opera arias.

I also enjoyed being outdoors. My dad assigned me to do several house chores like vacuuming the living and dining room carpets, cleaning the bathroom, kitchen, basement, and garage, and polishing his shoes. Although I didn't like doing this work and would often get in trouble by putting off my chores for as long as possible, I did like working outside in the yard for the most part. My job was to mow the front and back lawns, trim the hedges, and rake leaves. The one outdoor job I didn't like was weeding which I usually put off for as long as I could.

Because my dad was still concerned about my increasing isolation at school, he embarked on yet another self-improvement program like the Friar's Club. He thought this would ensure that I met other boys my age. So he persuaded me to join the Boy Scouts just after I had begun 7th grade and moved into my new home. I would take the long E Bus ride from 1457 Dana to St. Monica's where a Catholic Boy Scout troupe met in the evenings after school once a week. I stayed there for two years, eventually making it to First Class Scout. Although I still had a hard time making friends, at least I wasn't teased. And I did enjoy learning some new and non-academic skills such as tying knots and Morse Code. After I had been there two years, I had earned several merit badges. But my favorite Scout activity was camping. I remember how impressed my dad was with me for being one of the few boys to go on a winter camping trip once.

ST. MONICA
1957-58

However, my favorite memory from the time I lived at 1457 Dana, besides visiting Hannelore and Arnold Euler, was getting to know the Bourgeois family up the street from us. Dr. Joe Bourgeois was a fellow faculty member of my dad's at Xavier University. He taught French and German. His wife Jeanne came from Montreal and spoke French. Because of their mutual interest in foreign languages, my dad and the Bourgeois became close friends. Like the Harkins, the Bourgeois were a large Catholic family with eight kids. My dad would frequently baby sit for their younger kids. Or he would invite them to parties he now hosted at his new home.

As for me, I got to know the oldest Bourgeois boy – Pierre – and often went to his house to play. In college I also briefly dated their oldest daughter Marie. Later I took some of Dr. Bourgeois German language and literature classes. He quickly became one of my favorite teachers. I also got on well with his wife Jeanne, and I always felt welcome in the Bourgeois home. As an undergraduate, I joined the Heidelberg Club, a fraternity-like, German language club on campus that Dr. Bourgeois moderated. We met Sunday evenings once a month to drink 3.2 beer, sing German/Latin student songs like *Gaudeamus Igitur*, and listen to various speakers on German culture and customs. I was elected secretary of the club in my Sophomore year and vice president in my Senior year.

A few years ago, I had a unique encounter with someone who had known me in the 7th grade. His name was Al Lederer, and he found my name on the Internet. He emailed me: "Are you the same Anthony Wentersdorf I knew in 7th grade in Miss Junk's homeroom class whose dad taught English at Xavier University?" When I assured him I was, he told me that he remembered me as a quiet, soft-spoken, respectful, and intelligent kid whom he had admired for his outspokenness and courage. Apparently, I had stood up for myself concerning an issue I've forgotten about. Not only was it neat to reconnect with someone that far back in my life, but this unexpected development made me realize how tricky memories can be. When I asked Al if he remembered my 7th grade English teacher Helen Gerwig, he not only remembered her, but he told me he had kept in touch with her throughout the years. He informed me that she had married and was now living in Florida as a retired library director. He forwarded me her address, so I wrote her a letter. To my amazement, she indeed remembered me and the story

I had written in her class. So, this unexpected turn of events put an entirely different spin on this mostly troubled part of my life.

V – A Light in the Dark

I don't remember much about my junior high school years at Walnut Hills except that I was pretty unhappy there for the most part. However I had one unusual and unforgettable experience when I was about 15 years old that brightened up my life.

One of my dad's graduate students at Xavier University was a Catholic nun named Sister Mary Elissa who taught 7th and 8th grades in a parochial school in Covington, Kentucky. Somehow, Sister Elissa got wind of the fact that I was very unhappy at school. She therefore devised a unique plan that was to transform my life, at least for a brief moment.

So, she invited me to attend her eighth grade class for an entire week. She also persuaded the parents of one of her pupils, a troubled thirteen-year-old teenage boy named Ross, to let me stay with them while I was attending her classes. Fortunately, Ross took me under his wing and treated me like one of his buddies

I don't remember what I learned in Sister Elissa's class, only that she treated me like a very special guest. She encouraged me to share what it was like to grow up in Germany and to immigrate to America with my dad on an ocean liner. Not only did Sister Elissa make me feel welcome, but Ross and his classmates included me in all their activities and games. They invited me to join them in their pick-up baseball games after school. Ordinarily I would have been too scared to play because I was so inexperienced and awkward.

I hated 7th and 8th grade gym classes and was always the last one chosen for any team sports.

But here I felt accepted for the first time in my life and made to feel part of the gang. To my surprise, I quickly discovered that, despite my skinny build, I had some natural athletic ability that I never had a chance to develop. In my new friends' pick up baseball games, I was able to get some timely hits, although catching the ball was another matter. And no one teased me about being so skinny and awkward.

The week in Covington went by much too fast, and I didn't want to go back home. But the best was yet to come. On the final day of my stay,

Sister Elissa asked all the students in her class to write me personal letters expressing how they how they felt about me. I ended up receiving about thirty letters, all of them positive. The kids wrote me how much they enjoyed having me in their class. They liked hearing about my life in Germany and my exciting ocean crossing. They all saw me as intelligent, friendly, and likable. It was the first time I had ever felt accepted by my peers, even popular. It was a truly transformative experience.

When I got back to Cincinnati, I read those letters over and over until I knew them all by heart. They certainly helped relieve the loneliness I was feeling, at least for a while. I realized that I wasn't as unpopular as I had imagined myself. Even though my week in Kentucky didn't erase the trauma of my Walnut Hills years, they did give me a new perspective on my life. Yes, Sister Elissa had given me a wonderful gift that I would cherish for a lifetime and for which I would feel eternally grateful. My one regret is the fact that during my subsequent moves, I somehow lost all those letters. But the memory still remains.

AT ARNOLD'S AND HANNELORE'S

When I was going to high school, I was a troubled teen,
I tried so hard to find my way where I'd be heard and seen.
I didn't have that many friends and spent my time alone,
But I found a special place where I could feel at home.

At Arnold and Hannelore's, I felt that Christmas cheer,
And found that cosy feeling at their home each year.
At Arnold's and Hannelore's, the eggnog all flowed free,
As we opened up our gifts beneath the Christmas tree.

At Arnold and Hannelore's the kids showed me their toys,
Eric's Legos, Evi's dolls brought me a new-found joy.
At Arnold and Hannelore's, when all is said and done,
I felt part of their family and had a lot of fun.

VI – Glamour in the Mail

I was a late bloomer physically, emotionally, and sexually. I didn't start having strong sexual feelings until I was about fifteen or sixteen. But once puberty hit, it came with a vengeance! This was a serious problem because I was a student at St. Xavier, an all-boys' Jesuit high school in Cincinnati, where any kinds of sexual thoughts, desires, or actions were seen as mortal sins, punishable by eternal damnation in hell.

So, when I first started masturbating, I was constantly afraid that that I might be killed and go to hell if I didn't make it to confession in time. I would usually confess my sins on a Saturday afternoon, so I could be pure enough to receive communion at Sunday morning mass. But in my adolescent heart, I knew that I would probably sin again next week, and the week after that. After confessing the same sins over and over again to the same priests, I was afraid that they would eventually refuse to give me absolution because they saw me as a pervert.

In addition to my sexual guilt and shame, I was also extremely shy around girls. Except for Hannelore, my dad's best friend Arnold's wife, and Frau Stehmer, my dad's housekeeper, a very religious woman from Germany, who did our cooking and cleaning, I had very little contact with women or girls. Nor did I have any male friends to talk with about my emerging sexual feelings. And I certainly wasn't about to tell my dad. So, I gradually developed a secret double life which I worked hard to conceal from others.

One part of me was this quiet, studious, obedient boy who always worked so hard to please others and do well in school. The other part was the sexually starved, pubescent teenager who constantly fantasized about women's breasts and bright red lips. It didn't help matters that I was not only required to attend regular masses at St. Xavier High, but also had to attend an annual retreat in which our retreat master kept reminding us of the wickedness of sex outside of marriage.

But despite all this, my sexual urges became so powerful that they eventually overrode my guilt, shame, and fear of eternal damnation. As I got older, I found increasingly sophisticated ways to satisfy my fantasies without attracting attention. At first I clipped out newspaper ads showing women's dresses, make-up, and lingerie. Once I remember finding a Fuller Brush ad that our German housekeeper had left in the kitchen, which showed the face of astunningly beautiful, buxom woman with bright red lips and fine dark curved eyebrows. I managed to sneak it off to a secret hiding place where I could look at it later.

Around this time my dad subscribed to *Newsweek*, the back issues of which, he stored in a closet in the basement. When I knew that he would be out of the house teaching, I'd often sneak down to the closet to retrieve a whole bunch, and open them up to the ads depicting women's dresses, bras, and make-up. After piling the magazines around me, I masturbated myself into a blissful rapture, followed by intense shame, and fear that my dad might come back unexpectedly to catch me red-handed. Fortunately, he never did, but I had some close calls. I think I got some kind of perverse thrill out of leading this double kind of Jekyll and Hyde existence – on the outside this soft-spoken, well-behaved, ultra-polite boy who always got good grades and never got into any kind of trouble -- on the inside this raging sex-addict, consumed by dirty thoughts and wild desires that could plummet him straight into hell and eternal damnation.

My appetite for sexual materials escalated to the point where I sought out more stimulating pictures. I became increasingly drawn to beautiful women with big breasts, bright red finger nails, and full red lips. When the *Newsweeks and* newspaper ads proved too tepid, I sought out women's fashion magazines. But these were hard to come by since my dad didn't subscribe to such magazines, and I was too scared to buy them at the supermarket or drug store where I saw them displayed. I wondered what the saleslady at the checkout counter would think of a teenage boy who bought issues of *Cosmopolitan*, *Vogue*, or *Lady's Home Journal*. I assumed that they'd see me as some kind of pervert.

So, I devised another ingenious way of acquiring such a magazine. After spotting an ad for *Glamour* in the paper, I ordered a subscription to be sent to my home address. That way I wouldn't have to confront any saleslady. But there was one hitch. How could I be sure that I would be the first to pick up the mail when my Glamour arrived? For the next two weeks I sweated bullets, hoping to God that my dad wouldn't get to the mail before I did. I imagined his reaction:

"Tony, I noticed this women's magazine in today's mail with your name and address on it. Do you know anything about it? Surely, it must be some kind of mistake."

Fortunately, I was able to open the mail when the longed-for Glamour arrived. I quickly hid the magazine away in the safest place I could think of, and waited for the first opportune moment when my dad would be gone to work. Then I headed straight to the bathroom to unveil my new treasure. I spent the next hour in sexual bliss, frantically going through page after page of glossy photos of provocatively dressed women in all kinds of sexy poses, each one more tantalizing than the last. Some of them wore bras and my mouth watered at the sight of lots of ample cleavage. I masturbated over and over, no longer caring about hell or damnation.

My only fear now was of being caught in the act by my dad. What if he suddenly came back from work unexpectedly, and had to go the bathroom right away? I could imagine him asking me: "Tony, what's taking you so long in there?" Fortunately, that never happened, and I was able to safeguard my secret.

I remember many years later, when my dad and I could talk about these things more candidly, how he related an incident that showed me that he was more enlightened than I had given him credit for. It had to do with our German housekeeper, Frau Stehmer, who was a very pious Catholic. Once she had approached him looking very sheepish, and holding a copy of a *Playboy* magazine which she had found hidden under my mattress. She thought I had committed a terrible sin that my dad should know about, and that I should be punished for. However, he assured her that this was a perfectly normal thing for an adolescent boy to do, and just a typical part of growing up.

Of course I didn't know this as a boy of fifteen. After all, I was much too scared then to talk about sex with anyone, especially my dad. Who knows, but looking back, he may well have figured out about my *Glamour* subscription, but decided not to make an issue of it.

As I grew older and my sexual appetite increased, I craved more and more explicit materials. I was still too scared to buy women's magazines at drugstores or supermarkets. But every now and then I had a lucky break. Once, on my way home from school, I found a whole pile of women's fashion magazines in a trash can in an alley. I snuck them home and was in seventh masturbatory heaven for a month. Another time I found a large Sears catalog with pages and pages of lingerie ads showing women of all shapes and sizes clad only in bras and panties.

But the crowning moment of my adolescent sexual experiences came about in a most unexpected way. At the time, my dad and I lived in a house not far from the Xavier campus. We often spent Thanksgiving,

Christmas, and other holidays at our German friends Arnold and Hannelore Euler who now lived in an attractive apartment surrounded by woods in a Cincinnati suburb. Arnold's wife Hannelore subscribed to a number of women's fashion magazines that she ordered from Germany. When I turned sixteen, Hannelore gave birth to a baby daughter named Evelyn that I started babysitting for. So, every now and then on a typical Friday or Saturday evening, Arnold would pick me up to take me to their apartment, so I could look after baby Evi while they enjoyed a night out. While Arnold paid me a few dollars for my help, Hannelore showered me with lots of tasty treats and encouraged me to pick out anything I wanted from the refrigerator to snack on.

I soon began to look forward to these babysitting visits with a special kind of frenzied zeal that neither my dad, Arnold, nor Hannelore could have guessed at. This was due to a discovery I made one night after I had put little Evi to sleep. In a box in the living room I found her stack of German women's fashion magazines. Some of them were also scented with perfume which enhanced their sex appeal. And quite a few of the women were topless, something I had never seen in *Glamour* or other American fashion magazines.

On the first night of my new discovery, I had myself quite an orgy as I spread the magazines out on the living room floor while masturbating myself into a frenzy. This time I had no fear of my dad catching me in the act. My only concern was that little Evi might suddenly wake up and start crying, or that Hannelore and Arnold would come home early and catch me in the act.

After that night, I always looked forward to babysitting for the Eulers with a special fervor, now I had my own little secret that no one ever suspected. Nor was I was ever caught in my new-found wickedness. And the sexual thrills I got from these experiences more than made up for any feelings of guilt and shame I experienced.

VII – Stalag 17

Starting high school was an exciting new adventure for me, as well as a great relief, after my two years at Walnut Hills Junior High where I had been teased and bullied by some of the boys in my home room class. I had asked my dad to let me transfer to an all-boys, Catholic High School in Cincinnati, Ohio called St. Xavier whose teachers were all men, most of them Jesuits.

To get admitted to St. Xavier, I had to pass a rigorous entrance exam which determined in which class I would be placed for that year. Since my exam score was only average, I was placed in a middle-of-the-road class. During my freshman year I excelled academically, especially in Latin where I often got grades in the high 90s. This gave me a new kind of status with my classmates, but also caused me to be moved up into the top-level, honors class (2CC) in my sophomore year.

So, I went from being top of my class in my freshman year to bringing up the rear in my sophomore, junior, and senior honor's classes. I also drifted away from my first-year friends, and had a hard time making new ones. I had a hard time academically too, because, as an honor's student, I had to take the most demanding courses such as trigonometry, physics, Latin, and Greek. In my senior year, for example, we translated Virgil's *Aeneid* from Latin and *The Odyssey* from Homeric Greek. I'd often come home from school exhausted, only to face three more hours of homework.

Fortunately, I eventually did get involved in several extra-curricular activities. In my freshman year, I tried out for the school marching band since that had been one of my few positive experiences in junior high where I played the flute. But unfortunately, the St. Xavier Band had no flute to lend me, and I couldn't afford to buy one. The band director gave me the option of taking up the clarinet. But I didn't want to learn another instrument when I had already stared piano lessons.

I also tried out for the swim team. I had always loved the water and had learned to swim at the Y. Although I was a competent swimmer, I wasn't fast enough to make the varsity team. And there was no intramural alternative.

Still I didn't give up. In my sophomore year, I joined the poster club, an ideal activity for an introvert. I spent lots of happy hours after school making posters for various school events. I enjoyed forming letters and doing art work, though it didn't make me any new friends.

Around this time I also got involved in a classical music appreciation group moderated by one of the teachers. We met weekly after school to listen to classical records. Back then boys who listened to classical music were seen as "squares" by most of the students who preferred rock-n-roll. And the music itself was often called "that long-haired" music, probably because many of the past composers wore their hair long.

But that didn't faze the moderator who was able to instill us with the same love for the classical composers that he shared. He also taught us to listen in a new way. I learned, for example, that symphonies had four movements whose tempos and moods were described by Italian words like Allegro, Andante, and Scherzo.

I quickly fell in love with the symphonies of Ludwig van Beethoven, especially his *Sixth*, *Seventh*, and *Ninth*. I can still recall the jolt I felt at hearing the introductory "Da-da-da-dum" of his famous *Fifth*. And his *Ode to Joy* always sent chills down my spine. And when I discovered that he was completely deaf by the time he composed his *Ninth*, I felt an even stronger bond. I especially loved the Romantic composers because their passionate music resonated with the *sturm und drang* of my own adolescence.

Around this time I was also attending concerts at Cincinnati's Music Hall with its nationally acclaimed conductor, Max Rudolf. I have many fond memories of sitting up in the cheap, nose-bleed seats in my dark suit, listening to legendary pianists like Rudolf Serkin and Arthur Rubenstein, or violinists like Isaac Stern. My favorite pieces were the symphonies of Brahms, Tchaikovski, Mahler, and Dvorak. I'd often find myself following the conductor's animated hand gestures, or picking out members of the orchestra and imagining myself in their place.

There was one other extra-curricular activity I got involved with that had a profound impact on my life, but not the way I had hoped for. In my junior year I tried out and was accepted into the high school dramatics society. I had already seen some plays with my dad. I was convinced that getting up on stage and learning to act would boost my self-confidence, and help me overcome my shyness. The play that St. X was producing that year was called *Stalag 17*, a three-act comedy set in a German prisoner-of-war-camp during World War II. This play was later made into an award-winning movie starring William Holden, and also inspired the popular 60s' TV series *Hogan's Heroes*.

Although I was thrilled to get a role in a play, my excitement was dampened by the fact that I was cast as an SS guard because the director knew I could speak German. This unfortunate casting just served to reinforce my insecurity about being German. There was a further irony that this camp guard was supposed to be a big, intimidating figure who appeared at the beginning of ACT I, and whose job it was to wake up the barrack prisoners each morning with a bellowing shout: "Raus! Appell! Aufstehen! Mach schnell!" He did this while banging the prisoners' bunk beds with a night stick.

However, I was anything but intimidating. My skinny "ninety-eight-pound-weakling" body couldn't have scared anybody. And the helmet I wore was way too big for my head. But somehow, I managed to yell out my: "Raus! Mach schnell!" without embarrassing myself too much. To this day, I don't remember anything else about the play – how often it was performed, if the audience was receptive, or what kind of response I received. I was relieved, however, that my dad didn't attend any of the performances. After all, he had lived in Berlin during the 30s and 40s, and would certainly not have appreciated this unflattering depiction of Germans.

WHEN THE WORLD ALMOST ENDED

Dateline: October 1962

One week spent on the brink of eternity --

The Cuban Missile Crisis.

Who would blink first, Kruschchev or Kennedy?

The wrong move on this chessboard

Of life or death might mean

Virtual extinction.

Fortunately, we all stepped back

From the brink of the precipice,

And avoided Armageddon,

At least for the moment.

VIII – A Canticle for Leibovitz

While I was in high school, my father was invited by one of his colleagues at Xavier University named Joe to join a monthly book discussion group. Other members included Joe's wife Adelaide as well as a number of their friends, some of whom were middle-aged, unmarried women. Two of them taught voice and piano at the Cincinnati Conservatory of Music. Another worked as a secretary. They all took turns meeting at each others' homes on Sunday afternoons and evenings.

After a brief social time during which refreshments were served, the group would launch into a discussion of the book that had been selected that month. Afterwards, there was a break for dinner, and then the discussion would resume until around 9 or 10 p.m. At the end of the evening people would decide on the next book to discuss as well as where to meet the next month.

After my father had been in the group for about a year, Joe and Adelaide invited me to join even though I was still in high school. I think I was around fifteen or sixteen at the time. For me, joining the group proved to be a very welcome respite from the weekly grind of school since I was enrolled in a rigorous Catholic college-prep school where I had to do two or three hours of homework each night, taking courses in Latin and ancient Greek, translating Homer's *Iliad* and *Odyssey*, Caesar's *Gallic Wars*, and Cicero's *Orations*, as well as tough math and science classes like trigonometry, chemistry, and physics, not to mention advanced placement courses in English. So, it was nice to get a break from school and read books that I wouldn't be tested on.

Being in the group not only gave me a chance to be taken seriously by adults, but also provided me with a regular social outlet since I was still pretty much a loner and didn't really have any high school friends. I was very shy in social situations and found it hard to speak up in groups. For the most part, I stayed pretty much in the background. Once in a while one of the ladies might ask me: "How's school going, Tony?" Gradually, as I began to feel more comfortable, I would chime in every now and then with a comment or question.

One thing that struck me almost right away was my dad's confidence in expressing his views and regaling the others with stories from his life. This was due in large part to the fact that, as a respected college professor, he was used to speaking in public and presenting his views whereas I was not. I also noticed how he charmed the spinster ladies with his erudition and stories. But while they admired him, he was often dismissive of them. For one thing, most of them were quite homely. I remember one of them had buck teeth, the other a large ugly wart with hair growing from it.

I envied my dad's ability to socialize and resented the fact that he was often the center of attention, while I was relegated to the sidelines, tongue-tied and taciturn. Sometimes I'd start to feel more comfortable towards the end of the evening, even getting into brief one-on-one conversations with some of the women, but for the most part I had little to say.

Another thing that struck me was the difference in my dad's behavior once we got home when he often revealed a completely different side of his character. While articulate and outspoken in the group, at home he often turned withdrawn and uncommunicative. Or he would comment on some of the women's annoying mannerisms. One time he told me that he resented the fact that Joe and Adelaide were trying to fix him up with some of the single women in whom he had no romantic interest.

Usually, the meetings began with a discussion of the book that had been read that month, but often the political events of the day trumped the book discussions. One such time was while John F. Kennedy was running for president in the fall of 1960. I think all the women in the group had a secret crush on him. And the fact that he became our first Catholic president, endeared him to the group even more since everyone in the group was Catholic. I think we all celebrated when he was elected in November 1960. And everyone commented on the ignorance of those who were paranoid that Kennedy would be beholden to the Vatican once he became president. Two years later, our discussions became very animated as the world was on the brink of nuclear war during the Cuban Missile Crisis in October 1962.

And a year later, I recalled the endless, impassioned debates about JFK's assassination on November 22, 1963, including the various conspiracy theories that were making the rounds at the time. Did Lee Harvey Oswald act alone, or was he just a pawn in some sinister plot? How many shots were fired in Dealy Plaza? What was the link between Oswald and Jack Ruby? Was the assassination a Communist conspiracy? For example, people commented on the fact that Oswald had spent a year in the U.S.S.R before he shot Kennedy.

As the '60s wore on, these political discussions became more heated since we were all living in turbulent times. There were the Civil Rights marches in the South, race riots and burning cities, and anti-Vietnam student protests. I remember one book we discussed –John Howard Griffin's *Black Like Me*– about a white man who had his skin dyed black in order that he could document how blacks were treated in the South. Often our heated debates went on late into the evening, so that my dad and I wouldn't get home until eleven or midnight. Of course, I had to get up early Monday morning to go to school.

But most of the time, however, the discussions confined themselves to the books we had selected for that month. I don't remember most of them, but one of them stood out for me. That book was entitled *A Canticle for Leibowitz*. It was a dystopian, science fiction novel by an author named Walter Miller, and certainly one of the strangest books I had ever read. Maybe that's why it stuck with me for all these years. It was also very timely since it reflected much of the paranoia of the '50s and '60s, a time when school kids were taught to "duck and cover" under their desks to prepare for a possible nuclear attack, and when folks were constructing bomb shelters in their backyards. After all, the Cuban Missile Crisis was still fresh in everyone's minds, and the prospect of being annihilated by the Soviet Union was very real.

A Canticle for Leibowitz was set in the southwestern part of the U.S. in the near future after most of the country had been destroyed in a nuclear holocaust, and the remaining survivors had retreated to the Southwestern desert. They all lived a hermit-like existence and were trying to establish some kind of new world order. I think the novel appealed to me because its setting reminded me of the austere environment of my Catholic high school where many of my teachers were Jesuits who wore monk-like robes of black and lived an ascetic lifestyle. Since I spent so much time by myself, and didn't have any high school friends, the bleak environment and tone of the novel reflected the alienation and loneliness I was feeling at the time.

IX – First Jobs

With a few exceptions, I've never really enjoyed working, nor felt excited about job hunting. However, I began working for pay when I was still in high school. Before that I was already doing a number of unpaid chores assigned to me by my dad, such as vacuuming rugs in our living, dining, and bedrooms, cleaning the basement, bathroom, and garage, polishing my dad's shoes, mowing the lawn, clipping the hedges, and weeding.

While still a freshman at St. Xavier I got my first paying job working in the school kitchen for $.60 per hour sweeping and mopping floors and busing dishes. I did that for a couple of years until I got too busy with various extracurricular activities. During the summers I started mowing lawns for various Xavier University faculty families that my dad got me connected with. My salary now increased to $1.00 an hour. For the most part, I enjoyed doing these lawn jobs. I usually did them on Saturday afternoons. It felt good to be earning my own money for the first time in my life so I could treat myself to an ice cream or other treat. Besides mowing lawns, I also clipped hedges and did some weeding, something I already had a lot of experience with. I remember one woman I worked for – a Mrs. Link – who had a large backyard as well as a swimming pool which she sometimes asked me to clean by skimming the surface of the water with a filter. I kept on doing these lawn mowing jobs throughout high school and into my college years. Most of the people I worked for had some connection to Xavier University. Of all the early jobs I've done these were my favorite.

One of the more unusual jobs I got when I was a high school junior was working at the Xavier University church –Bellarmine Chapel– as an assistant sacristan. This involved preparing the various priestly vestments – albs, chasubles, and surplices – for daily mass. This job paid me $5.00 a week and required a just few hours a week. It supplemented my lawn mowing work. I remember that my priest supervisor – Father Manning – was a dour, taciturn man who hardly ever spoke a word. I did this job until I graduated from high school.

Another more unusual job was working at fur coat store called Friedman's, sorting various women's fur coats. I don't remember much about this job, how much it paid, or how long it lasted, only that I found the store environment to be stifling and confining. I still remember the musty smell of some of the coats.

By the time I started college as an undergraduate, I got my first "real" job working at the McDonald Xavier University Library. I don't remember how much I earned in this job, only that it was more than $1.00 per hour, but not by much. I used my earnings to help me pay for books and dorm fees. I started out working for a skinny, tall, soft-spoken librarian named Mr. Wall. The first place I worked in was an ancient-looking building with several floors. I worked in the periodicals department, and my job was running up and down the steep dark stacks retrieving journals and periodicals for patrons. I did this for about two years until a new library building was erected. My job then switched to working in circulation, helping patrons check out books, periodicals, and other materials. This time I had a different boss that I don't remember anything about. I worked there part-time for about 20 hours a week, continuing until I graduated from college.

I liked doing library work for the most part. It wasn't too stressful, and I often had time to do my own reading when there was a lull in patrons' requests. Plus I loved being surrounded by books. It was neat to be able to do my homework while getting paid for it.

A GOOD CATHOLIC BOY

He was such a pious boy,
Who went to mass each day,
Knew his Latin prayers by heart,
And watched the priest transform
The wine to Christ's own blood.
He believed in Jesus, Mary,
And the saints and angels too.
Confessed his sins each Saturday,
To Communion Sunday morning.
But something happened
Then along the way,
As the pieces of his faith no longer fit.
He was made to feel
Ashamed of his body's needs,
So his passion turned to guilt,
And made him fall away
Into fear and doubt,
As the firm foundation of his creed
Crumbled into dust.

X – Growing Up Catholic

For me, growing up Catholic was a very mixed blessing. I remember being very pious as a boy. I had my first communion at the age of seven in Germany. I spent the summers after my mother's death at Father Joseph Albingers, my dad's Catholic priest friend who had spent several years imprisoned in Dachau Concentration Camp. I stayed at his parsonage in a little German village called Poppenhausen. I also remember playing "mass" with one of my older friends when I was in second grade. While he played priest, I was the altar boy. Later on, while attending various parochial schools in Cincinnati, I was an altar boy, which was then called a "server." I continued as a server during junior High and High School, learning to say the Latin responses while the mass was still in Latin.

While attending St. Xavier High, I attended daily mass every morning before classes started. I also went to mass on Sundays at Bellarmine Chapel on the Xavier University campus. And once a year, all of us boys were required to attend a weekend retreat at a Jesuit Retreat House outside of the city. Most of my teachers were Jesuit priests who wore long black cassocks. For the first few years of high school, before puberty hit, attending a Catholic school and going to mass presented no problem since I didn't question my faith.

However, once I began to experience my emerging sexuality, my situation changed a hundred and eighty degrees. I began to feel a lot of shame. Since the priests saw any kind of sexual fantasies, desires, and actions outside of marriage as sinful, things became increasingly difficult. Not only was masturbation viewed as a mortal sin, punishable by eternal damnation in hell, but any kinds of sexual desires and thoughts were also seen as sinful. As a result, my visits to the confessional increased exponentially, since we weren't supposed to receive holy communion if we had committed a mortal sin.

Therefore, I usually had to go to confession every Saturday afternoon before I could receive Communion with a clear conscience on Sunday. Attending daily mass at St. Xavier also presented a problem because I was now masturbating frequently, always scared of going to hell if I got hit by a car or died in an accident.

During my high school years at St. Xavier, I had mixed feelings about attending those required retreats. They were usually held at a Jesuit Retreat House about twenty miles outside the city. All of us boys stayed there from Friday evening until Sunday afternoon. We would attend prayer services on Saturday and mass on Sunday morning. But the highlight of the weekend was the Saturday afternoon lecture-sermon which was given by the retreat master in the chapel.

On the one hand, I looked forward to these sermons because the priests would often regale us with compelling stories about the life of Jesus and the New Testament. They knew how to hold the boys' attention. It was also the time of Vatican II with its many reforms initiated by Pope John 23rd whom I really liked because of his liberal views. I remember one year when the retreat master told us about the famous shroud of Turin, a burial cloth discovered in the early 20th century, that dated back to the first century A.D., and was supposedly the cloth that Jesus was buried in. The shroud bore the bloody marks of the nails on the hands and feet of a man who had been crucified, as well as the spear wound on the side, the scourge marks on his back, and the crown of thorns on the head. This shroud was revered as a holy relic by the church. I also remember how the priest emphasized the scientific accuracy of this discovery. What made these sermons all the more interesting was that we were studying ancient Roman history, as well as translating Latin texts like Cicero and Caesar in school, so it made those times come to life.

On the other hand, I also dreaded those sermons because the priests always stressed the importance of keeping the 6th commandment – "Thou shalt not commit adultery!" They warned us boys about the evils of sex outside of marriage, that having any sexual thoughts and desires was a mortal sin. They also dwelt at great length on the passion and death of Christ on the cross. I remember one priest's description of the scourging of Our Lord in graphic detail – how the whips used were tipped with jagged pieces of metal so they would inflict added pain on Christ's back. One priest stressed the fact that every time the boys masturbated, or even had a sexual thought or desire, he would be driving the nails deeper into Christ's hands and feet.

During these retreats, I would usually go to Confession on Saturday afternoon so that I could receive Communion on Sunday morning. Since I was masturbating regularly by then, I lived in constant fear of going to hell before I could get to confession.

When I started college at Xavier University at the age of 19, these retreats continued. But by now I was becoming more and more skeptical, starting to shed at least some of my guilt. But I'll never forget one retreat that I attended in my sophomore or junior year in college. It was held at a Trappist monastery in Northern Kentucky called Gethsemanie where the famous monk and author of *The Seven Story Mountain* – Thomas Merton – had lived. I got there on a Friday evening and stayed until Sunday afternoon. I remember that we weren't allowed to talk at all except during prayer time and to say the responses at mass. All our meals were all held in silence. That wasn't so bad since I still felt shy around the other students and often didn't know what to say.

But the hardest part of the retreat happened to me during one of the nights after evening prayers when I went to bed in my tiny cell-like room. I remember I had a hard time going to sleep because at home I always had the radio on so I could listen to music. But this time there was absolute silence. I had a scary nightmare Saturday night and when I woke up, the ticking of my clock seemed so loud that I thought I was going crazy. I couldn't sleep the rest of that night, and was very glad to get back home on Sunday to resume my normal routines.

By the time I finished college, I had stopped attending daily mass or those annual retreats. I was gradually drifting away from my faith and becoming an agnostic. There was at least one benefit to this. I could now masturbate without experiencing intense guilt and shame, although it took me many more years and much therapy before I could let go of these feelings entirely.

XI – Driving Lessons

My dad didn't buy a car until the early 1960s. Before that, he was quite content to get around by bus, and reluctant to invest in a car because, as he reasoned, he had lived in Germany all these years where he had never needed a car, so why buy one now? However, his friend Arnold, who had already bought himself a bright pink Chevy Bellaire in 1958, finally persuaded him to purchase his first vehicle. It was a modestly priced, compact, beige-colored Chevy II. I remember that my dad never enjoyed driving, doing so only when he had to, for example, to go shopping, or visit the Eulers and Stehmers. Since his new home was so close to the Xavier campus, he was able to walk to work.

Fortunately, there was a small one-car garage built into the basement of our house, so that my dad didn't have to leave the car parked on the street. That would have been dangerous since our house was situated on a sharp curve on the road. I'd often hear the squeal of tires as cars speeded along Dana Avenue as they hit the bend in the road. I still remember one car that didn't make it. It missed the curve and ended up on our front lawn.

Whereas most of my high school classmates were learning to drive at the age of sixteen, I had no such desire. In fact, I was terrified at the prospect. Finally, when I turned nineteen, had started college, and we'd had our car for about three years, my dad thought it would be a good idea for me to learn how to drive so I could become more independent and self-sufficient. But I was very reluctant because I was scared I might have an accident.

But eventually, my dad prevailed as he usually did. He found the name of a driving school where he signed me up for lessons. I don't remember much about those lessons except that I was a very nervous student. My instructor was a young man in his 30's who sat next to me on the passenger side while I took the wheel. I was a very cautious driver. I was especially scared of making left turns. And parallel parking proved to be an obstacle too. I must have taken lessons for about three of four months, I don't remember exactly, meeting once a week for an hour. My instructor had me drive in traffic right away so that I could overcome my fears. I surprised myself when I passed the driving test on the first try, even though the tester took off a lot of points for parallel parking.

After passing the driving test and getting my driver's license, I felt an enormous sense of accomplishment. This freed me up to become more independent. I could now help my dad by running various errands or going shopping at the supermarket for groceries. During the summer after my sophomore year in college, I actually moved away from home for the first time to live in a college dorm. It was the coach house of a former mansion that had been converted to a dorm for Xavier honor's students. I moved into the second floor of the coach house to live with a Chinese student majoring in philosophy named Peter Ma. He was my first roommate. I'd often end up giving him rides to places he couldn't get to by bus. Gradually, I got so used to driving that I actually started to enjoy it.

However, there was one major mishap that almost ended up tragically.

During the summer after my sophomore year in college, my dad decided to take a vacation by driving out east to North Carolina. He had heard from a friend that Cape Hatteras on the outer banks of the North Carolina coastline was a beautiful vacation destination. It was located near Kitty Hawk where the Wright Brothers made their first successful flight in December 1903. So my dad decided to take our Chevy II cross-country.

At first, everything went smoothly as my dad and I shared the driving, spelling each other every few hours. But then, somewhere near Roanaoke, Virginia, we had a near-fatal accident. I was driving at the time. It was dusk, and we were cresting a hill when I didn't see a car that was heading straight for us. Before I could react, the speeding car crashed into us head-on. I remember coming to a abrupt stop and bumping my head on the steering wheel. Even though I wasn't seriously hurt, I was in a state of shock. My body was trembling uncontrollably. Fortunately, neither my dad nor I were hurt except for a few bruises. But out Chevy was damaged pretty badly. So, we left it in a Roanoke garage to be repaired. My dad decided to rent a car so we could continue our vacation trip. Fortunately, we had no further mishaps.

I'm really glad we didn't abort our trip. We both had a really good time. My favorite part was walking along the many sand dunes along the coastline and swimming in the Atlantic. I also enjoyed visiting the Wright Brothers' museum where we saw a replica of their plane. On the way back, we were able to pick up our repaired car and proceed uneventfully back to Cincinnati. For me, it was certainly an unforgettable vacation in more ways than one!

XII – A Shot in the Dark

Although I didn't do any dating in high school, I did develop a crush on a girl named Anne Feldhaus. Lou Feldhaus was a friend of my dad's who also taught English at Xavier University. His specialty was modern drama, and he was involved in the Xavier University dramatics club, The Masque Society. Mr. Feldhaus, his wife Huberta, and their two children Anne and Joe lived in a large, old rambling house on top of one of the seven hills that form a ring around downtown Cincinnati.

I remember the house well because it always reminded me of one of those many-gabled haunted houses in movies like *House on Haunted Hill*, or the House of the Seven Gables in Emily Bronte's novel *Wuthering Heights*. While I was in high school my dad would often drive his Chevy II to the Feldhaus home on Saturday or Sunday afternoons. I always enjoyed those visits because my dad and Lou Feldhaus had some heated discussions about the theater and various actors they both admired while Huberta served us refreshments. They also had an old upright piano in their living room on which I often improvised melodies while the grown-ups talked.

But the best part of my visits was getting to know their daughter Anne. She was four years younger than me, but mature for her age. She was also a bit of a tomboy, so we'd often play in their large backyard climbing trees or playing badminton. While in junior High and during my first years of high school, I still had no interest in girls, and Anne and I were just good buddies. But by the time I reached my senior year in high school, I had developed a crush on her. I remember carving the initials of her first name on a battered old table in our back yard while doing homework. Pretty soon my main interest in visiting the Feldhauses was to see Anne. Of course I was much too shy to let her know how I felt about her. So my love remained very platonic. I would never even have dared to hold her hand, much less venture a kiss.

By the time I was nineteen and had learned to drive, I would sometimes drive my dad's car to the Feldhaus home so I could visit with Anne. When I started college, I joined the Xavier University Marching band where I played the flute. One time I invited Anne to a party our band was having in the campus Field House. But once I got there, I was so shy I didn't know what to talk about. That put a damper on further dating attempts, at least for a while. But whenever I played piano pieces like Beethoven's *Moonlight Sonata* or Debussy's *Claire de Lune*, I would get into a romantic reverie and imagine holding hands with Anne.

After the band party debacle, I made one more serious dating attempt. By now I was 19 years old and a freshman in college.

Since I had just gotten my driver's license, I invited Anne to go to a movie with me in downtown Cincinnati. I picked her up in my dad's Chevy II and drove to the movie theater. The film was a Peter Sellers comedy called *A Shot in the Dark* – one of the Pink Panther series. I thought its light comic tone would put us both in a good mood and dispel the nervousness I felt around her. I was sure we'd at least get some good laughs. And I wouldn't have to worry about what to talk about once the movie started.

At first, everything went fine. The film lived up to its promise and made both of us laugh, relieving the tension between us. I got a kick out of the outrageously bizarre antics of the bumbling detective Inspector Clouseau as he constantly put his foot in his mouth, or tripped over himself, while flirting with the ladies. I also got a big kick out of his heavy French accent. I felt certain that I had chosen a good "date" movie, and that everything would now go smoothly.

But then I was thrown for a loop. Suddenly, in the middle of the movie, the scene shifted to a nudist colony where Inspector Clouseau was chasing down one of the suspects. I turned red as a beet, my delight suddenly transformed into intense embarrassment. I did not dare look at Anne, wondering what she thought of me for inviting her to see such a risque film. I squirmed in my seat for the rest rest of the movie. And by the time it had finished, I felt so ashamed and embarrassed that I hardly dared to look at her. Nor did I know what to say, whether to apologize or to change the subject. As a result, there was an awkward silence on the long drive back to her home. I abandoned any hopes of dating Anne again, assuming that she wouldn't want to go out with me again. We drifted apart and I stopped visiting the Feldhaus home for many years after that.

Eventually, I got over my crush. Nor did I go on any more dates during the rest of my college years, preferring to socialize with my men friends. It wasn't until I started graduate school at Ohio State four years later that I had my first real girlfriend and fell in love for the first time.

PART III
At Home and Abroad

THE NIGHT THE HITS KEPT COMING

The night the hits kept coming,
I found my first new friends
In the world of rock-n-roll.
The Beatles, Dylan, Stones, and Beach Boys
Serenaded me that night,
As I woke up to a whole new world
Of sound and music.
My life would never be the same
After that Thanksgiving night,
And I would start to grow
In ways I never could have guessed.

I – A Pop-Rock Epiphany

In the summer of 1986, I was riding home to Minneapolis with a friend after having played some music at a St. Paul park. I noticed that he had his radio tuned to an AM station that played the songs of the '50s, '60s, and early '70s. The DJ was calling them classic rock. Not only was that the first time I had heard this term, but also the first time I had heard these songs in almost twenty years, not since attending college in Cincinnati and Columbus, Ohio. Listening to them sent shivers up and down my spine, and rekindled the old excitement I felt when I first discovered this new kind of music.

As soon as I got back home, I found this classic rock station on my radio, and for the next week, listened to it every chance I got. I felt a kind of rebirth as I relived my college memories. I rediscovered all my old friends – The Beatles, The Rolling Stones, The Mamas and Papas, The Doors, Simon and Garfunkel, The Moody Blues, The Beach Boys, The Bee Gees, and many more.

While growing up in Cincinnati, Ohio, and before that in Germany where I was born, I knew next to nothing about jazz, pop, or rock-n-roll music. My dad didn't have a radio, and he listened only to classical music. I cut my teeth on Prokovief's *Peter and the Wolf*, Moussorgsky's *Pictures at an Exhibition* and Debussy's *Claire de Lune*. I grew up on the arias of Enrico Caruso and John McCormack, the symphonies of Tchaikowsky, Brahms, and Beethoven, and the operas of Verdi, Puccini, and Wagner.

I was briefly exposed to another kind of music while attending Junior High at Walnut Hills High School in Cincinnati where I joined the marching/concert bands to play the flute. They performed themes from popular Broadway musicals like *West Side Story* and *Oklahoma*. But it wasn't until I attended college in the mid-sixties that my musical horizons would expand in a totally unexpected way.

In the fall of 1966 during my junior year at Xavier University, I had a chance to move into a beautiful dorm called Marion Hall, located just off the Xavier campus. To me it seemed more like a mansion than a dorm since it had been the residence of a wealthy family before Xavier purchased it. Next to it was a coach house where the servants used to live and keep horses and coaches. I got a chance to stay there with three roommates in a big room on the third floor. The room had high ceilings, large windows, and a fireplace. There were two bunk beds for the four of us.

Marion Hall was the residence of the Xavier Honors Bachelor of Arts (HAB) students. They, being the cream of the crop academically speaking, were required to take all the toughest university courses such as Latin and ancient Greek, zoology, chemistry, physics, and calculus. The only reason I qualified to live there was the fact that I had been accepted into the HAB program during my freshman and sophomore years. But in my junior year I dropped out because the academic requirements were just too difficult for me.

I'll never forget my three roommates though. There was Wayne Cowens, the tallest and brightest of the bunch. His brother Dave was a well-known basketball star for the Boston Celtics. But Wayne was a serious student. He was a math major who maintained a 3.92 grade point average throughout his four years in college, winning summa cum laude honors upon graduation. Then there was Bill Hale. He was a short, mousy-looking guy who was also a math major, but not in Wayne's class. He "only" got a 3.25 grade point average (still cum laude). But Bill's heart wasn't in his studies. He preferred doing more fun things like listening to the radio, playing all-night monopoly games, watching late night TV, and doing magic tricks with his best friend Gene.

And that brings me to my most charismatic and unforgettable roommate, Eugene H. Castillon. Like his friend Bill, Gene came from New Orleans where, like me, he had attended a Jesuit high school. He had received a full four-year tuition scholarship to attend the HAB program at X. U. and was now completing his senior year as an English major. Although not as intellectually brilliant as Wayne,

Gene was able to effortlessly maintain a 3.5 average over four years. He also belonged to the university's Honor's Society. But unlike Wayne, Gene didn't restrict himself to cracking the books. Although he did well in his studies, he had more than enough time left over to pursue his many hobbies and side interests. And that's what drew me to him. We soon became good friends as I gradually found myself drawn into his multi-faceted world.

I was amazed at all the things Gene found time to do. He was a member of The Mermaid Tavern literary society as well as editor of *The Athenaeum* literary magazine. Although skinny like me, he loved to pig out on pizzas, and once won a student pizza eating contest in which everyone was amazed at how many pizza slices he could pack into that slender body of his! One day, long before jogging was as popular as it is today, Gene introduced me to running after telling me about the pioneering book on that subject –*Aerobics*– written by Dr. Cooper, which touted the benefits of aerobic exercise. So, it wasn't long before Gene had me accompany him on his runs through the streets of campus and the city.

Gene also had some more unusual hobbies. One time he made a home movie at Marion Hall using an 8 millimeter camera in which his dorm-mates played all the roles. He loved watching late-night, classic horror movies on our basement TV, and introduced me to the likes of the Werewolf, Frankenstein, and Count Dracula. He also introduced me to Johnny Carson's *Tonight Show* which he watched every night before going to bed. Then there were those all-night card, Monopoly, and Clue games we played on weekends. Sometimes, Gene would buy a supply of monster make-up, and once scared an unsuspecting, gullible dorm-mate half to death by knocking on his door wearing a monster face.

Where Gene got the time to do all this and still excel in his studies, I'll never know. But he gave me a clue once by telling me how he managed to figure out what his college professors wanted on tests and papers, then giving it to them. However, Gene's most unusual interest was an obsession. He was an amateur magician. He and his friend Bill both belonged to a national magician's fraternity called IBM (International Brotherhood of Magicians. Two of his heroes were Harry Houdini and Harry Lorayne, a well-known stage mentalist and memory expert.

It didn't take long before all the other Marion Hall residents knew about Gene's obsession. When I returned home from my Xavier classes, I'd often find him sitting on the landing steps demonstrating his latest magic tricks to a captive audience. Except he preferred to call them "effects." It wasn't long before I too became drawn into his world of magic and became a willing guinea pig. Gene loved doing card tricks the most, but he also did rope and coin tricks, as well as mentalism acts. One of his favorite phrases was: "Pick a card, any card...." Two hours later, I'd still watch him do Faro shuffles, or find a mysteriously missing card in my wallet. The most frequently used word in Gene's vocabulary was, "Amazing!"

Yes, as I got to know Gene better, I was amazed at the extent of his creative talents, and all the things he could pull off. I learned, for example, that Johnny Carson, our favorite TV talk show host, had been extremely shy as a young man, and had started out as an amateur magician. No wonder Gene liked him so much.

So, that was our Marion Hall gang during my glorious junior year. For me it was a great experience in many ways. For one thing, I got better grades than during any other semester at Xavier. It was also my first full year away from home, I had found my first close friend, and I was happier than I had ever been.

However, this leads me to the heart of my story. Besides Wayne, Bill, and Gene, there were two other important personalities in our dorm room. These were Wayne's and Gene's radios. Wayne's was a large old-fashioned set that was usually tuned to the classical music station. In fact, it was one of the first public radio stations in the country called WGUC and located on the University of Cincinnati campus. Since Wayne was usually the first one to get up weekday mornings, I'd often wake up to the strains of Vivaldi's *Four Seasons* or a Bach fugue.

Gene's radio was a completely different story. He owned one of those small, new-fangled, battery-operated transistor radios that young people were using all across America. He had it on almost constantly while studying or doing his homework. Sometimes he wore headphones, but more often than not, I could hear the strange new music pouring from it. It was usually tuned to WSAI or WUBE-AM, two top-forties stations. The music pouring out of it was definitely not classical, but the new rock-n-roll that was transforming the lives of youngsters everywhere, the kind of music I was totally ignorant of so far.

At first, this new music stayed mainly in the back of my consciousness, so I didn't pay much attention to it. Nor did Gene ever say anything about it. I think for him it just was just background noise to help him concentrate on his studies. But for me it had an exciting, dangerous quality that I became increasingly drawn to. I sensed it was the kind of music my dad would not approve of, nor my professors at Xavier. Actually, Wayne's classical music seemed a lot safer and more familiar. Yet, through some strange, unconscious process of osmosis, I was gradually absorbing these new sounds during my first few months at Marion Hall.

During the Thanksgiving holiday of 1966, my three roommates traveled back home to their families -- Wayne to Boston, and Bill and Gene to New Orleans. I decided to stay back in Marion Hall by myself. It was no big deal because my dad's home was just a twenty minute walk from Marion Hall. I visited him and some family friends on Thanksgiving Day, but spent the rest of the time alone in my Marion Hall dorm room. I loved having the whole place to myself since most of the other HAB students were gone for the Thanksgiving Holiday. That meant I could come and go as I pleased, watch any TV shows I wanted. It also gave me time to catch up on some course work and term papers, at least that's what I told myself. I really cherished my new-found freedom of which I took full advantage!

One evening, it may have been Friday or Saturday, I just sat back in Wayne's big easy chair and let my imagination wander off to where it wanted to go. Suddenly, I remembered Gene's radio and the strange, thrilling rock-n-roll songs that had intrigued me for the past three months. At first, I was afraid to turn it on because I thought Gene might be upset if he found out I had tinkered with it, and because it seemed somehow forbidden. I was sure that by listening to it I'd be breaking some commandment. I also had visions of our dorm proctor, a Jesuit priest named Father Felten who lived in the dorm, storming into my room and shouting, "Turn off that infernal noise!" But my fears were unfounded. Nothing of the sort occurred.

It was just me, the big empty dorm room, and Gene's radio. Finally, I got up the guts to turn on his set. Sure enough, it was tuned to WUBE where they were doing some kind of 1966 Hits Countdown. Gradually, I turned the volume up until it filled the room with sound. Of course, I often checked outside my room to make sure nobody was coming. But the coast remained clear. So, I just sat back in my easy chair and let the new sounds wash over me. What a big thrill! I felt as if I was discovering a whole new world that I'd been cut off from all of my life.

At first, I had no idea of what to make of the new songs I was hearing since I didn't know any of the names of the groups, singers, or song titles. But I felt myself drawn to some songs more than others. In my head I developed a rating system similar to the grade point averages I was familiar with in my college courses. I gave my favorite tunes four points (the number assigned to an "A"), three points ("B") to good songs, two points to average songs, and one point to songs that just didn't make the grade. Of course, the music was often interrupted by annoying commercials, but every now and then they had an intriguing spoken segment about this brave Chicago crime fighter named Chicken Man, who could stop criminals dead in their tracks. "Chicken Man! He's everywhere! He's everywhere!" the DJ kept repeating.

As I sank back into my chair, and evening turned into night, I was drawn further and further into these new songs: "Baby, everything is all right, uptight, out of sight! ... da, da-da-da, da-da-da ... I can't get no satisfaction, I can't get no reaction, but I try, and I try, and I try ... Hey, ninety-eight-point six, it's good to have you back again, oh, hey ... Here comes my baby, here she comes now, and it comes as no surprise to me with another guy, no matter how I try-yyyyyy ... She would never say where she came from, yesterday don't matter when it's gone ... Here comes the sun, na-na-na-na, here comes the sun, oh I say, it's all right." As I set there mesmerized, chills running up and down my spine, the hits continued, and I was discovering a new world I never knew existed. From that moment, I knew my life would never be the same. I wanted to hear more of this thrilling new music.

In the meantime, ol' Chicken Man kept me abreast of his crime-stopping adventures in Chicago. "Chicken man! He's everywhere! He's everywhere!"

And as the countdown to midnight continued, the hits kept coming: "In Penny Lane there is a barber showing photographs of every head he's had the pleasure to have known ... Hey, Mister Tambourine Man, play a song for me in the jingle-jangle morning I'll come following you ... But it's all right now, Jumping Jack Flash, it's a gas! ...There is a house in New Orleans they call the Rising Sun ... Hey, you, get off of my cloud! ... Do you love me? ... Hello, I love you, won't you tell me your name ... Everybody's gone surfin,' surfin' USA." And on and on and on, all night long!

By midnight, I no longer worried about anyone barging in to complain about the loud music in my room. As the countdown went to 9-8-7-6, I turned the radio up another notch and completely abandoned myself to the music. "5-4-3-2-1 ... And now for the number one hit of 1966!" ... then another battery of commercials and another adventure from Chicken Man. I don't even remember what the number one hit was, but I'm sure I must have given it a 4+ rating. I don't think I went to bed until three or four the next morning. I may even have stayed up until dawn. As I finally tried to get some sleep, these new songs kept spinning around in my head. One thing I knew for sure, that by the time I got up the next day, I was a different person. In fact, a part of me never wanted to wake up, never crack the books again. I was suspended in a new kind of nirvana that only a twenty-one year old can experience!

But of course, wake up I did. And life went on as it must. The Thanksgiving weekend ended. Wayne, Bill, and Gene returned. I kept attending classes, writing term papers, and taking tests. That spring, my three roommates graduated, and I was on my own again.

I graduated a year later in 1968. But I will never forget that thrilling, enchanting November night in 1966, sitting in Wayne's armchair, listening to Chicken Man's adventures and the cascade of rock hits that transformed my life forever!

1968

Where were you in 1968?
Where were you, oh where were you in sixty-eight?
Were you on time, or were you late,
Passing through that Golden Gate?
I saw lots of people rioting in city streets of hate,
With others dragged out on drugs, moving from state to state,
They were sending our boys across the sea
To a bloody, senseless war.
A Kennedy and a King got shot,
Seemed peace would come no more.
Hope sprang new on campuses as students demanded their say,
They wouldn't be pushed around by draft boards and old ways.
Beatles, Dylan, and Rolling Stones sang a generation's songs,
While Sergeant Pepper's Hearts Club Band had us join along.
When I look back to those days, I remember when
With all my hopes and ideals, everything seemed possible then.
So, here's to 1968 and all it meant to me,
Some things I sure wanna forget, some to keep in memory.

II – Where Were You in '68?

1968 was certainly a year to remember! It was a year of major upheavals and strife, a year of multiple changes and shifts, a year filled with political dissent, multiple assassinations, and violent demonstrations worldwide. It was also the most exciting year of my life till then.

Things got off to a bad start in early April when Martin Luther King, then only 39 years old, was assassinated in Memphis, after he had rallied striking garbage collectors to stand up for their rights. Not long after that, president Lyndon Baines Johnson elected not to run for office again that fall because of the increasing unpopularity of the escalating Vietnam War. And in June, things went from bad to worse when presidential candidate Robert Kennedy was killed by Sirhan Sirhan at the Democratic Party headquarters, shortly after he had won the California Primary.

Nor did things get any better during that long hot summer. The Democratic Party Convention in Chicago turned out to be a bloodbath in which peacefully demonstrating students were brutally attacked and beaten by Chicago cops unleashed by Mayor Richard Daley. There were also violent anti-war demonstrations all over the world, including in Berlin, Rome, and Tokyo. And by the time the November presidential election came around, a weakened Hubert Humphrey was narrowly defeated by Richard Milhouse Nixon who escalated the Vietnam War even further and ushered in his Silent Majority.

My own life that year was also full of multiple changes and adventures. However, most of these were more positive. Sometime in early spring, I was classified 1A by my draft board and assigned to appear for a physical at the Cincinnati Draft Induction Center. Fortunately, because of my persistent psoriasis, I was declared unfit for active military service and given a 1Y status, which kept me from having to go to Vietnam, and meant I would only have to serve in case of a national emergency. That was certainly a great relief, although I don't remember much about this chapter in my life. But my dad made sure to remind me.

In June 1968, I completed my B.A. Degree at Xavier university with double majors in English and German, as well as minors in French and Philosophy. With a cumulative grade point average of 3.22, I narrowly missed out on receiving Cum Laude honors. However, during my commencement exercises I found out that I had received the Xavier Poetry Prize for my sonnet *Metamorphosis*. I was also awarded The

Heidelberg Award for attaining the highest grade point average in my German language and literature classes. But my crowning achievement was winning the Fredin Scholarship to study French that summer at the Alliance Francaise in Paris along with fourteen other Xavier students.

Traveling to Paris was certainly an adventure of a lifetime! I spent that summer with my 14 fellow Xavierites in a Paris student dormitory while studying French language, civilization, literature, and phonetics at The Alliance Francaise. However, that summer wasn't all work and study. We were treated to some fine meals at various Paris cafes, bistros, and restaurants. We also went on numerous city sight-seeing tours, and spent a whole week on an extended bus tour, visiting the world-renowned Cathedral of Chartres, and several *chateux* (castles) along the River Loire. I still remember that spectacular *son et lumiere* (sound and light) show at Chenancaux, during which I learned the story of that palatial castle after being treated to a fine seven-course meal.

My Paris stay turned out to be even more of an adventure than I had bargained for because, just before our arrival, the entire city had been shut down by a strike of workers and students protesting President DeGaulle's conservative political ideas. By the time we got there, students were battling it out with armed security police on the streets of Paris. I witnessed several demonstrations in which people fled the police into the subterranean entrances of the Metro to keep from getting beaten or tear-gassed. Fortunately, none of us were seriously hurt, but we were all pretty shaken up by these events.

When I got back to the States, there were more big changes in the wind. That spring, I had applied for graduate assistantships and fellowships at several prestigious universities like The American University in Washington D.C. and The University of Illinois in Champagne-Urbana. I was helped by the fact that I had scored in the 91st percentile on the Graduate record Exam. I was delighted to find out I was awarded a full four-year PhD fellowship to study English literature at The Ohio State University in Columbus, Ohio. This was a dream come true! And to make things even better, Ohio State was only a two-hour drive from my Cincinnati home. That way I could easily keep in touch with my dad and Xavier friends.

So, full of optimism and excitement at my future prospects, I enrolled at Ohio State and moved into Steeb Hall, a graduate dorm on campus. I began taking courses in Old English, Beowulf, and Chaucer. I soon made new friends in the dorm, including two Jewish grad students from Brooklyn, New York, as well as a fellow Catholic student from Manhattan. Yes, John, Elliott, Don and I spent all of our spare time hanging out together, sharing meals in the student dining hall, and playing cards and ping pong. Don soon became my best friend.

However, the biggest thrill and joy of my life was yet to come! While studying Old English grammar in the graduate library one day, an attractive young woman in my class sat next to me. She introduced herself and suggested we get together to study. Her name was Patricia Werblan. She told me that her grandparents were Ukrainian, and that she had grown up in Lorain, Ohio, not far from Youngstown. Like me, she was a grad student in English. And like me, she had fallen in love with the French language. She had taught French in an elementary school, as well as having had an astonishing variety of other jobs. She was also a year older than me.

Since I was still extremely shy around women and had hardly done any dating, I couldn't believe that an attractive, experienced woman like Pat would take an interest in me. But she took the initiative in starting a dating relationship. Before long, I found myself falling head-over-heels in love with Pat, and spending every spare moment with her. I soon introduced her to my dorm friends John and Don, spent many hours listening to Judy Collins and Simon and Garfunkel records at her rooming house, and talking about everything under the sun from politics to music. Pat was the first person that I felt comfortable sharing feelings with. She was also a great listener. We soon grew to love each other very much.

In December I went home to Cincinnati to visit my dad for Christmas. I'll never forget the profound joy I felt for being in love for the first time in my life. What a great way to end an already extraordinary year! Yes, 1968 was certainly a year to remember! Unfortunately, that was all to change in 1969.

III – Combien Coute-t-il?

For me, it was a dream come true! A chance to go to Paris for the first time in my life to study French literature with fifteen other scholarship students from Xavier University where I had just gotten my bachelor's degree.

At twenty-two, it was to be the adventure of a life-time. Even before I arrived in the City of Lights, history was already being made. In

May of '68, all of Paris was in an uproar. The city was on strike. The Sorbonne was shut down while students and workers joined to hold protest demonstrations in the streets. They erected concrete barriers, and threw paving stones at the police who were armed with clubs and large, see-through, plastic shields. The police, in turn, reacted violently, lobbing tear-gas canisters, chasing protesters down Metro entrances, beating them with clubs, and even shooting some with live bullets. The entire city was in crisis!

By the time I arrived with my other fourteen fellow Xavier students at the end of June, things had calmed down a bit, but students and police still fought it out from time to time, and lots of innocent people got caught in the cross-fire. I saw people running down Metro entrances, and getting trampled to get away from the security police who were lobbing tear gas canisters after them, or clubbing the ones who couldn't get out of the way fast enough.

There was another problem. My French classes at Xavier didn't prepare me to make myself understood with the actual people I'd meet there. I assumed they would be mostly French, or other tourists like myself. The women in our group were in for an especially rude awakening. Most of them had attended all-women's Catholic colleges, and were totally unprepared to deal with the ultra-aggressive behavior of some of the Arab men from Algeria, Morocco, and Tunisia they met. Many of these men hit on the women by pressuring them to go to their apartments for "a good time."

At first, I was swept up by the excitement of it all. After my experiences in arch-conservative Cincinnati where I had attended eight years of Jesuit schools, I was ready for a big adventure. I felt liberated for the first time in my life. And these daily scenes of street riots and general mayhem increased my adrenaline rush.

One thing that struck me immediately was the aura of overt sexuality all around me. Everywhere I looked, there were flashy billboards with beautiful women dressed in fashionable dresses and wearing sexy make-up. I saw young couples kissing, necking, and making out in parks, sidewalk cafes, boulevards, and Metro stops.

I knew that Paris was the city for lovers, but I had never anticipated anything like this. Talk about raging hormones! In Cincinnati, the Legion of Decency was still banning books like *Catcher in the Rye*, and boycotting old burlesque theatres.

Eventually, I found a room in an old university dormitory on the outskirts of Paris called the Cite Universitaire. I spent my mornings taking classes in French language, literature, culture, and phonetics at the Alliance Francaise language school with the others in our group. In the afternoons, I'd hike up to Montmartre, map in hand, take in an organ concert at Notre Dame Cathedral, check out the paintings at the Louvre, or take a bateau mouche boat tour along the Seine. Sometimes I'd join some of my classmates for a lunch of a baguette, some camembert, and a bottle of *vin ordinaire* (cheap wine) at an outdoor park.

Occasionally, our group went on longer excursions. In mid-August, for example, we took a whole week off from school to visit the spectacular castles along the Loire river. For me, the highlight of that trip was a visit to a beautiful chateau called Chenanceau where we were served an seven-course feast right inside the castle. The tables were lit with candles and the roof was hung with chandeliers. I had so much champagne and cognac to drink that night that I lost all my inhibitions. I ended up talking a mile a minute with my college friends. After dinner, we were treated to a uniquely French kind of entertainment – a *son et lumiere* (sound and light) show. The entire castle was lit from the outside while ghostly voices related the castle's bloody history from inside its walls.

However, there were two disappointing things about Paris stay. One was the fact that I hardly met any real Parisians. Most of them left Paris in the summer to vacation in Provence and other southern vacation spots. So, I ended up trying out my mangled French on the other Americans in my group, or the foreign students I met at the Alliance Francaise.

The other had to do with my raging hormones. Although I was very shy around girls, had hardly done any dating, and was still a virgin, I longed for some kind of transcendent love experience. I fantasized being seduced by some beautiful, experienced Parisian woman, preferably older, who could teach me all the arts of love, French style. But this was not meant to be. Some of the more assertive men in our group did manage to date some French girls. And most of the women in our group were approached by men. But the only women I got to know were other, sexually inhibited foreign students like myself. Still, my hormones raged on unrequited.

One weekend, I thought that my dreams would finally come true. My roommate John planned to celebrate *Le Quatorzieme Juillet*, (French Independence Day) in a big way. He invited me to join him, his French date, and her American girlfriend to see the holiday festivities. He had brought along plenty of wine, cheese, bread, and pastries. We met with the two women to watch the big afternoon holiday parade. Afterwards, John invited them into our dorm room. He and his date were in great spirits. The wine was flowing. But I and the other woman were very uncomfortable around each other. I was much too shy to approach her, and had no idea what to say, or how to proceed. I kept waiting for her to make the first move. But I wasn't even attracted to her because she was both plain and unfriendly. Yet, I still longed for some kind of sexual experience.

However, she took an instant dislike to me. While John and his date spent the night sleeping together, the other woman and I hardly spoke a word to each other, and ended up spending the night sitting in separate chairs, dozing off. It was one of the most frustrating nights I had ever experienced. The next morning, when the women left, I was so depressed, I ended up skipping that day's classes.

However, the rumor of John's exploits quickly spread to the other students in our group. For the next few days, they gave us significant winks, especially the men. Little did they know how how wrong they were about my part in this whole affair. The only thing I felt was a lot of shame and frustration.

As the time of my Paris stay drew to an end, my pent-up sexual cravings grew stronger. Finally, out of sheer desperation I decided to act on my own. John had told me about Paris' infamous Red Light district on the right bank of the Seine in a run-down area called Les Halles. It was there where vendors sold wholesale produce every morning around dawn.

So, early one morning in late August around 2 a.m., I ventured out of my dorm, making sure no one would see me. Clutching a folding Paris map in one hand, my stomach tight with excitement and fear, I took the Metro from my dorm to the right bank and started wandering around the Red Light District. At first, I didn't see anyone since it was so late. I figured that all the prostitutes had already quit for the night. But then I began to see a few heavily made-up women lurking around street corners and under lamp posts. I didn't see any men. I was so nervous that my hands were shaking. I spent what seemed like an hour just wandering around the streets, too scared to approach anyone for fear of getting beat up by some thugs.

But finally, I bit my lip and walked up to the first woman I saw. I don't remember much about what she looked like because it was still dark, and

I was so nervous. But I could tell she was somewhat plump, unattractive, and middle-aged. I asked in the best French I could muster, "Combien coute-il?" (How much does it cost?)

I don't even remember her answer. But to my complete surprise, she abruptly took my hand, gave me a patronizing look, and escorted me to a small shabby hotel nearby, up a narrow flight of stairs, to the second floor. There on the landing stood an old beat-up, wooden desk manned by a uniformed, mean-looking man in his forties who nodded brusquely. The prostitute then told me in broken English that it would cost me 100 francs, and motioned that I should hand my money to the concierge sitting at the desk. Even though I had saved this money for the rest of my Paris stay, I now quickly handed it over to this scary-looking guy.

The prostitute then motioned me to step into her tiny room. I remember it had a bed which took up most of the space, a small table, a chair, and a bidet which I'd never seen before in the U.S.

At first I just sat there on her bed, paralyzed by fear, not knowing what do do next. Finally, she gave me a funny look and asked me, "Etes-vous puceau?" I had no idea what she meant. I'd never heard that word before in any of my French classes. Giving me a look mixed with pity and scorn, she repeated. "Are you a virgin?" Instinctively I answered: "Oui, I mean, yes, madame." Then she countered: "I don't do it with virgins."

Now, for the first time, rage trumped my fear. I felt she had no right to treat me this way. I replied: "I want my 100 francs back since you won't provide the service I paid for."

"You are not getting any money back!" she replied indignantly in her broken English. "You already paid me. But I don't do it with virgins. Do I not make myself clear? I don't do it with virgins! Voila! Now, if you don't leave right now, I will have the concierge throw you out. Comprenez-vous?"

She didn't have to ask me twice. As fast as my anger had surged before, it now disappeared, replaced by fear, shame, and loathing. I got out of that room as quickly as I could, avoiding the concierge. I stumbled down the narrow stairs, and practically ran out of that hotel, relieved by the feel of the fresh air on my face. I never looked back. Nor did I approach any more prostitutes.

Instead, I slowly made my way back home, walking the entire distance. By the time I got back to my dorm room at the Cite Universitaire, the sky was already turning pink with the approach of dawn. I never mentioned this experience to anyone in our group, nor anyone else, for that matter. I felt it was my secret to keep. I knew that I had experienced more of an adventure than I had bargained for, and that I had had a significant coming of age experience, a certain loss of innocence, from which there was no turning back.

MY SEAGULL GIRL

She was my seagull girl, but I lost her long ago,
She flew away from me to find another way to go.
She brought me warmth and sunshine,
Brightened the darkest night,
She fed the flickering flames of love
Till they grew emerald bright.

We walked and talked the hours away,
Explored each other's hearts,
Like babies fresh upon the world,
We never stayed long apart.

And now she's happily married
With a son and a bright new home,
But I'll never forget the times we shared
As long as I got to roam.

IV – 1969 – Up in Smoke!

In 1969, things didn't get any better in our country than they had in 1968. President Nixon expanded the Viet Nam War to include his Christmas bombing of Hanoi and a military incursion into neighboring Cambodia. Anti-war demonstrations multiplied as National Guardsmen invaded college campuses with tear gas, billy clubs, and bullets. Things came to a head in the spring of 1970 when four students were killed at Kent State University.

After King's assassination, Detroit, Chicago, and other inner cities erupted in violence as angry black mobs looted, burned, and destroyed their own neighborhoods. King's philosophy of non-violence was quickly replaced by the violent dictates of Malcolm X and the Black Panthers.

In 1969, my own life took a decided turn for the worse. It didn't happen all at once, but gradually by degrees, starting almost imperceptibly at first, but eventually increasing to a torrent of multiple changes that I felt powerless to prevent. Looking back now, I realize that the seeds of this paradigm shift were sown much earlier, but I wasn't able to see them coming until it was too late.

From the time I began my graduate studies at Ohio State, a part of me wasn't really that excited about my course work. But I just went along because school was all I knew how to do. I never gave much thought to where it might lead, or what would be the next step. I was just so excited to have gotten that four-year fellowship. I thought that everything would just work itself out in the end. I felt relieved not to have to look for a job, a prospect I dreaded. I enjoyed hanging out with my new friends at the dorm. And falling in love for the first time in my life was even more wonderful that anything I had hoped for.

My first quarter classes went well. They weren't any more demanding than some of the HAB classes I had taken as an undergraduate. Learning Old English grammar and translating Beowulf reminded me a lot of my Latin and Greek classes at Xavier. They didn't require much original thinking, just translating texts, something I was good at. I also enjoyed the easier class schedule. Instead of five or six three-credit classes a semester, I now only had to take three five-credit classes per quarter. Instead of having to attend classes three or four days per week, I managed my fall schedule so that I only had to attend classes two mornings a week. Thus, I was lulled into a false sense of security.

But by the second quarter, when I still hadn't made any friends in the English Department, and felt even less enthusiasm for my classes than I had the first quarter, my grades began to head south. Instead of the straight A average I had gotten in the fall, I now received Bs. And Dr. Stevens, my graduate adviser, who taught some of my most important classes, expressed some concern about the downward trend. But instead of applying myself more rigorously towards my studies, I began to lose interest in my course work, spending more and more time hanging out with my friends, playing cards, and spending time with Pat.

My first major set-back occurred sometime in February 1969 when, unbeknownst to me, Pat started dating some other guy on campus. It took me a while to catch on to what was going on because I was so naive about these things, and didn't want to accept that Pat might fall out of love with me. But one day, she told me that she had gotten "hung up" on someone else. Eventually, she started dating my friend John. When I found out, I was completely surprised and totally devastated. I didn't want to believe that my first love would dump me for one of my best friends. This not only made spending time with John and Don more painful, but also plunged me into a deep, dark depression.

Keeping up my grades in my Chaucer and Old English Prose classes now became even more difficult. Because I hadn't been able to really make any other close friends, I continued to hang out with John, Don, and Pat, painful as that now was, rather than be by myself. Somehow, I was able to get through another quarter's worth of courses. But my heart was no longer in it.

What made things even worse was the fact that, in contrast to my situation, Don was doing so well in his industrial psychology classes. He had made new friends in his department, was excited about his studies, and would often regale us with stories about his professors, fellow grad students, and class projects. I, on the other hand, had nothing to say about my English classes and professors. So, I couldn't help comparing myself with him.

The one bright spot in all this was the fact that Pat still wanted to be my friend. In the spring, she encouraged me to take up the guitar, telling me about a folk guitar teacher named Mike who had taught her to play. She encouraged me to take his non-credit folk guitar class where I learned to play songs by Bob Dylan, Simon and Garfunkel, and Tom Paxton. I bought myself a cheap, used, six-string folk guitar and played it every chance I could. I also bought myself record albums of folk musicians like Judy Collins, Donovan, and Phil Ochs. Learning to play guitar helped to soften the blow of losing Pat, while giving me something else to take my mind off my increasingly frustrating classes. I was also happy to join Pat and my friends John and Don in all kinds of fun activities. Thanks to Pat's initiative, we went to a campus coffeehouse called The Cockroach to hear local folk singers. One of my highlight concert experiences that spring and summer was hearing Peter, Paul & Mary. I also heard a very talented blind bluegrass guitar player named Doc Watson. Hearing them perform opened up the new worlds of folk music and bluegrass.

Besides the guitar, I also got involved in some other extra-curricular activities like The French Club's theater production of Moliere's play Le Medecin Malgre Lui where I attended a few rehearsals and got a small part. I even went to some meetings of a local Hare Krishna group. Anything to get away from my classes. By the end of spring quarter, my interest in my studies had diminished so much that my grades fell even further. I did the absolute minimum work to get by, spending most of my time playing cards with Don, John, and Elliott, playing my guitar, or attending concerts and free campus events with Pat.

Eventually, my graduate adviser, Dr. Stevens, called me into his office to let me know that I had lost my four-year PhD fellowship due to my falling grades. He told me I could still complete my Master's degree and apply for a graduate assistantship in the fall. He also encouraged me to take his summer course in medieval drama. But my grades would have to improve for me to continue in grad school. Not only did I find my classes dry and boring, but I still hadn't made any friends in the graduate English department. I dreaded having to write term papers which often determined most of my grade. I dreaded giving oral reports even more, and was deathly afraid of having to stand up in front of a class of seminar students to deliver a report on subjects I could care less about. I had to force myself go to the library to digest all those scholarly books and periodical articles I needed for my research papers. I hated having to substantiate my research with endless footnotes. By now I was really floundering badly academically. All I wanted to do was play the guitar and sing those folk songs I was falling in love with.

However, with one final last-ditch effort, hoping against hope that I could still succeed despite my better judgment,I followed Dr. Steven's advice to enroll in his medieval drama graduate seminar that summer. It was a desperate move. My entire grade depended on an oral report and final research paper. I found both to be excruciatingly difficult. Giving the report was so traumatic that I remember nothing about what I said, only that delivering it in front of those 10 seminar students was agonizingly painful. I was sure that they all regarded me as totally incompetent. The only positive thing was the relief I felt when my report was done. Writing the paper was just as painful. I put off doing the research for as long as I could. Then I managed to cobble together some half-baked ideas from various books and journals at the last minute. I spent all night before the paper was due typing up the final draft, while John was also working on a paper for one of his classes.

I wasn't surprised by when I only received a C-. I knew that this was tantamount to a failing grade for a graduate student. A few days later Dr. Stevens summoned me into his office. He told me how disappointed he was, not only in my below-par performance in my paper, but in my falling grades throughout the past year. He thought I had a fine mind and lot of potential that I just didn't put to good use. As for my paper, I not only used a lot of outdated source materials that had already been discredited by reputable scholars, but I failed to present any of my own ideas to reinforce my arguments.

Then came the clincher! He suggested that I drop out of school altogether to pursue some other line of work. A part of me was thankful that he gave me a way out. But another part of me was terrified because school was all I knew. I had no idea what other kind of work I could do. And the prospect of job hunting terrified me. Around this time, I was offered a couple of other options. I could sign up to take a written comprehensive test, which, if I passed, would at least enable me to get an MA. Or I could return in the fall as a teaching assistant, which meant I would have to instruct two freshman English composition classes in the fall quarter while pursuing further graduate studies. But the prospect of having to face two classes of 30 to 40 students each, scared me even more than dropping out of school to get a job.

How could I possibly teach a ten week class from scratch, face a classroom of students, and grade all those papers when I could barely do an oral report in front of ten graduate seminar students, or write a successful research paper? I did end up taking that written comprehensive exam in faint hopes of at least getting my Masters degree. But even that was not meant to be. When I failed that test too, I was told I would have to wait a year before I could take it again.

By now I felt like a total failure! Any dreams of continuing my four-year fellowship and becoming an English professor like my dad were shattered. I had lost the only girl I loved. Soon I would also lose my dorm friends John and Don because I had to leave the campus in the fall. I was now headed into a very uncertain, scary future, forced to do the very thing that scared me the most – look for work.

RETURNING TO MY ROOTS

Returning to my roots,
To the town where I was born,
Finding a new home
When I was split and torn.

Finding my new family,
That I thought I'd lost,
Finding a new place to live,
Melting all the frost.

A foreigner in my home town
Where I had my birth,
A new place I could lay my head
Upon this welcoming earth.

V – 1970 – Returning to My Roots

So much can change in the span of just one year. While at the beginning of 1969, I was floating on a cloud, by the end of that year my fortunes had completely reversed. In January 1969, I was in love, getting to know new friends in the graduate dorm where I lived, on a four-year

Ph.D. fellowship, and getting straight A's in my courses. However, by the end of that year, my girlfriend had broken up with me, I had lost my fellowship, flunked my Master's exam, dropped out of school, and moved back to my hometown in Cincinnati.

In September 1969, I got a job working as a packer at Rosenthal Printing Plant in a seedy part of downtown Cincinnati. This proved to be quite a comedown from the sheltered life I had experienced in college and grad school. By January of 1970, I was feeling thoroughly deflated and demoralized, forced to work at a job that felt totally alien. And what a job! After going to school all of my life, my body just wasn't used to the physical grind of blue-collar labor. My job was to grab newspapers and magazines as they rolled off the huge printing presses onto a conveyor belt, and stack them onto skids. Being young and agile, my body soon got acclimated to the physical strain of the work.

But what was much harder was the psychological adjustment. Instead of being with fellow students with whom I had an intellectual rapport, I was now toiling side by side with a bunch of rough-looking, tough-talking blue collar working men who liked to swear, look at girlie magazines, and kid around. Some of them thought it was strange that a college grad would be doing this kind of work, and teased me about it. But fortunately, I wasn't bullied, and they gradually accepted me since I worked hard. My body eventually got used to the grind of working the 11 p.m. to 7:30 a.m. graveyard shift. It also helped that one of the guys I worked next to was a black Vietnam vet who took me under his wing and prevented me from being razzed by some of the other men.

Around this time I got a cheap, tiny room in a kind of boarding house for working men. But I missed my grad school friends, especially my former girlfriend who had broken up with me the year before. I was very lonely and spent most of my free time consoling myself with my guitar which I played every chance I got. As my job dragged on without any hope of a change in fortunes, I got increasingly depressed until I finally made a decision to look for something more suitable. But I was hampered by my fear of job hunting. I remember that one snowy morning after getting off work around 8 a.m., when I made a decision to quit this thankless job and trust that I could find something better. It felt so good to finally take charge of my life instead of feeling like a passive victim.

So, in March 1970, I did find another job working as a credit clerk at a Sears and Roebuck store. That lasted for about a month. Then I saw a

Help Wanted ad for the position of copy clerk at the premier Cincinnati Daily, *The Cincinnati Enquirer.* I was elated at the prospect of finding work that related to my education as an English major. Unfortunately, the pay was very low, even less than I had been earning at the printing plant. And the hours weren't much better since I had to work from 5 p.m. until 2 a.m. the next morning when the early editions of the paper were delivered. But at least now I was employed in a more white collar environment with reporters and editors.

It didn't take me long to adjust to the routines of my new job which involved taking copy from the wire service machines, reporters, and editors on the upper floor, and sending it via pneumatic tubes to the linotype operators in the basement. I remember the day in early May when I clipped a breaking story from the UPS wire service about four students killed by National Guard troops at Kent State. As much as I liked working at *The Enquirer*, however, the pay was so inadequate, even less than I was paid at Rosenthal Printing, that it was barely enough to cover my living expenses. So I was forced to seek new work. Fortunately, however, fate intervened on my behalf when I got a job I had applied for that spring.

I had sent out two important job applications. First, I applied to become a Peace Corps volunteer since I found out that they were looking for college graduates who could teach English overseas for two years. That seemed like an ideal opportunity because I had always dreamed of working overseas, especially after my summer in Paris. And that way I could put my language skills to good use. Second, I found out that Switzerland was looking for Gastarbeiter (guest workers) to work in Zurich that summer. I didn't hear any more from the Peace Corps, but in May I received a letter that I was accepted as a guest worker at The Locanda, a Swiss-Italian hotel-restaurant in Zurich. At first, this seemed like a dream come true. I would now be able to live and work abroad and use my German language skills to best advantage. Although this job didn't pay that well, it did provide me with free room and board.

Thus, I embarked on a new adventure that I could never have anticipated. However, the work itself proved every bit as taxing as my printing plant job had been. For the first couple of weeks I worked as a waiter at The Locanda. But after a couple of weeks, I was demoted to *passe-platier* , or a glorified bus boy. My job involved carrying trays of cooked meals from the chef and cooks downstairs to the restaurant upstairs, as well as busing dirty dishes. It meant spending most of the time running up and down the stairs whenever a new order was ready. It took my body awhile to get used to all that running, but eventually I got pretty good at it, and even won the respect of the chefs and cooks.

However, I had one surprise in store. I thought I'd be able to use my German language skills, but they were of little use since the Swiss restaurant staff didn't speak the high German I was used to, but a dialect known as Schweizerdeutsch, which I barely understood. That summer, I ended up speaking a lot more English than German since that was the common language of most of my fellow guest workers. They came from all different countries in Europe, and some from the U. S. I met young men and women from England Ireland, Yugoslavia, Turkey, and Italy. Soon cliques began to form of people from similar countries who hung out together. Since I was pretty shy, I didn't really get to know anyone that well except two gentlemen from Malaysia, both of whom spoke English. We became good friends and often got together after work to take walks, or explore the city and its attractions. However, when I wasn't working, I spent most of my time playing guitar and harmonica. I purchased a six-string folk guitar and several harmonicas at music store in downtown Zurich and spent many hours singing songs of Tom Paxton, Judy Collins, Donovan, Peter, Paul, and Mary, Simon and Garfunkel, and Bob Dylan. I even found a Swiss-American folk music club that met in the evenings where they played British and American folk songs.

When my job ended at the end of August, I decided to take a couple of weeks off to travel in Switzerland, Belgium, Holland, and Germany. My dad happened to be vacationing in Europe that summer, so we met up in my hometown of Marburg in order to visit my aunt Lucie and cousin Alice. It felt good to meet up with my dad, and it was exciting to see my aunt, whom I hadn't seen since I was a boy in Germany.

I also had quite an adventure during one of my excursions. I traveled to Amsterdam to see the Anne Frank House. I had read her diary in college and found it very moving. There I met up with a young American woman who persuaded me to smoke some hashish. At the time, Amsterdam was known all over Europe for its easy availability of drugs. What I really was hoping for was to sleep with her, but she was more interested in the drugs. Unfortunately, after taking a few puffs of the cigarette she offered me, I took an instant dislike, and had no desire to smoke again. After the girl and I parted ways, I had no further misadventures.

As soon as I got back to the States, I found a letter in the mail from The Peace Corps informing me that they had tentatively accepted me as a possible volunteer, and invited me to fly out to Denver, Colorado, all expenses paid, for a final staging interview. I was overjoyed with the prospect of working as a Peace Corps Volunteer . I found out that they were planning to send me to Seoul, South Korea to teach English at one of their universities. But, alas, it was not meant to be. I failed the final interview of which I don't remember much, except that one of the questions the interviewer asked me was: "Are you gay?" I must have given them the wrong answer because that was the end of my Peace Corps dream.

So sure was I that I'd be accepted by the Peace Corps, that I hadn't made any alternate plans. I knew that I didn't want to return to the printing plant, or reapply for another copy boy job at *The Enquirer*. However, an alternative solution gradually suggested itself, thanks in large part to my summer visit with Tante Lucie in Marburg. What if I were to return to my hometown in Germany to live with my aunt, and work and study in Marburg?

So, that's what I did. My dad thought it was a good idea too. Fortunately, Tante Lucie was happy to have me stay with her on a temporary basis until I could find a place of my own. So, in September 1970, aged twenty-five, I embarked on a new adventure which would change my life forever. I would return to my roots, back to my hometown of Marburg where I had been born and lived until the age of five. I moved into Tante Lucie's small upstairs apartment on the outskirts of Marburg. I'll never forget that train ride from Frankfurt to Marburg along the rolling hills of Hessen, past quaint little towns and villages with their stone houses and church steeples that dotted the landscape. A part of me felt like I was coming back home even though I didn't remember much of growing up there since it had been so long.

Tante Lucie welcomed me warmly, and I felt an immediate affinity with her because she, like me, was a gentle soul with an artistic temperment. She was also a good cook. And she loved flowers which she grew on the window sill of her living room. Since she didn't speak a word of English, I was forced to speak German immediately. She also let me sleep in her daughter Ali's room. Ali was a year older than me and working on a Ph.D. in African Studies in Hamburg. She only came home on holidays.

My first challenge was to better my knowledge of German which was pretty rusty at the time. Even though I could understand most of what was said, my speaking ability wasn't that good, and I lacked a lot of vocabulary words and colloquial expressions. So, with Tante Lucie's help, I enrolled in a local language school for non-German speakers called Das Lessingkolleg which I attended until Christmas.

My next challenge was to do the very thing I hated most -- look for work, since I couldn't expect Tante Lucie to provide me with free room and board. I found out about an agency called Hilffix which offered temp jobs like gardening, translating, and tutoring. One of the first jobs I got was helping someone move. That was back-breaking work which fortunately lasted only one day. I applied for a job translating materials from German to English. I thought I'd have a good chance at getting that job since my dad was a translator before he became a college professor, and I had had a double major: English and German. To see if I could do the work, my prospective employer gave me a highly technical, scientific text on the subject of geology to translate from German into English. I had to look up practically every word in the dictionary, and had a hard time understanding even the English words, much less translating them from German. It made me realize how much I needed to learn before I could consider myself fluent. Fortunately, I was able to find several gardening, weeding, and lawn mowing jobs. So all the work I'd done as a college student mowing lawns came in handy. I enjoyed working outdoors. But even those jobs were only temporary and usually didn't pay that well.

Fortunately, Tante Lucie came to my rescue. She was working at a Marburg library at the time whose director she knew. She put in a good word for me, told him about my library experience in the U.S., and was able to get me a full-time position working at the Marburger Staatsbibliothek Preussischer Kulturbesitz. This was a large research library that had originally been located in Berlin, but whose holdings had been transferred to the undamaged town of Marburg after the war. The director who hired me, Dr. Rister, was a big JFK fan. I think that may have influenced him in hiring me in the first place. So on November 1, 1970, I began work as a full-time *angestellter* (library clerk) at the Staatsbibiothek, a large, impressive, red brick building in downtown Marburg on the Universitaetsstrasse, the main street in the center in Marburg. Although my pay was considerably more than I had ever earned in the U.S., the work itself proved less than inspiring.

My job was to copy catalog entries from various periodical indexes onto small catalog cards. If I was hoping for public contact and reference work, I was sorely disappointed. I sat in a large room at a long table next to about half a dozen other clerks who were doing similar work. Working full-time proved to be hard on me physically. I had to sit all day in a stuffy, badly-lit room, doing tedious, repetitive, detail-oriented work. It made me long for those lawn mowing and hedge clipping jobs I'd gotten through Hilffix. The one saving grace was that I got to know several fellow employees who sensed that I was unhappy, and reached out to me. One warm lady named Esti invited me to join her and some of the other clerks for their short morning tea breaks. I also got to know one of the part-time employees who sat next to me, an attractive, friendly, outgoing young woman named Gitte.

Another thing that made my new job bearable, was my good rapport with Tante Lucie whom I found to be very welcoming and sympathetic. I also enjoyed my evening classes at Das Lessingkolleg . It felt so good to be increasing my fluency in both spoken and written German. I also met a couple of young women at the school whom I dated briefly.

Just before Christmas, Tante Lucie's daughter Ali came home for a visit. Right away I noticed how different she was from her mom. Whereas Tante Lucie was soft-spoken, polite, and apologetic, Ali was prickly and highly critical. She found my inadequate German language skills amusing. She also thought I was lacking in table manners. So, one evening during dinner things came to a head! I was feeling extremely tense, hurt by a disparaging remark Ali had made about my manners, feeling rage swelling up inside, but too scared to voice my displeasure. Then, suddenly, the dam of pent-up emotions burst as my fork flew from my plate, almost hitting Ali in the face. Ali broke out in hysterical laughter. Fortunately, no one was hurt. But the incident helped to relieve the tension that had built up between us.

After that incident, my relationship with Ali improved considerably and we were able to come to a guarded understanding. I did appreciate all her help. For one thing, she encouraged me to enroll at the Marburg University – Die Phillipps Universitaet. She helped me fill out the required forms, and encouraged me apply for student housing in a dorm complex near the campus, since she didn't think it was wise for me to live at her mom's for too long. I agreed with her on that point since I was eager to be out on my own and get to know other university students my age.

That Christmas with Tante Lucie and Ali was one of the happiest I can remember. Tante Lucie bought us a beautiful Christmas tree which Ali and I helped decorate. Then she prepared a delicious meal of roast duck. Since I was earning so well, I was able to buy both mother and daughter some nice gifts. So, on *Weihnachtsabend* – Christmas Eve – we all sang German Christmas carols, opened our gifts, took pictures, and toasted the season with a bottle of Sekt – champagne. Tante Lucie and Ali also introduced me to some German Christmas traditions they didn't have in America. One ritual called Bleigiessen involved melting pieces of lead with a lit candle, and dropping the molten lead into a tub of water where they were transformed into interesting shapes. We then tried to guess what the shapes meant, and what they might portend for the coming year. And on New Year's Eve – *Sylvesterabend* – I witnessed another German tradition as Lucie and Ali set off some fireworks from their apartment balcony. We all had a wonderful time, and I faced this New Year with a lot more optimism than I had the previous one.

I ended up living in Germany for the next two and a half years. Early in 1971, I moved out of Tante Lucie's apartment into a student dormitory near the university campus. I also changed my library job from full-time to part-time, so I could enroll in classes at the Phillipps Universitaet. I even sought out psychological help for the first time in my life, and started attending a weekly therapy group to help me with my depression. Yes, my life was about to change again in many positive ways.

In hindsight, I'm glad I didn't get that Peace Corps job after all, since then I wouldn't have gotten to know my aunt and cousin, regained my fluency in German, gotten to know some good new friends in the dormitory, or become re-connected to my roots.

EBENEZER TOULEASSI

Ebenezer Touleassi,
Where are you today?
Are you back in Togo,
Land of your birth,
Ministering to the afflicted?

Ebenezer Touleassi,
Your name sounds like the sweet songs
You sang and played on your guitar,
Or like the lovely tapestries
You hung on your dorm room walls,
That transported you back home.

Ebenezer Touleassi,
Such a good friend to me
In Marburg when I was floundering.
I almost lost you then,
But will always remember you now
For the gifts you gave me.

VI – A Foreigner in My Own Home Town

The next two and a half years would mark an important turning point
in my life. I would spend that time living, studying, and working
in my hometown of Marburg. After leaving Tante Lucie's home in
Ziegelstrasse in the winter of 1971, I moved into a student dormitory
called Vilmarhaus on the other end of town, that was run by the
Lutheran Church. I stayed there for the next two years.

Vilmarhaus was a beautiful, new, white dormitory complex with one
tall building and two smaller ones. At the time I moved in, its three

buildings had just undergone a major shift called a *Gemischtbelegung,* a change to a co-ed facility. This was done by the students themselves despite the church's initial objections, and floors that had previously been segregated according to gender, were now co-ed. I would benefit from this change since one of my neighbors was an attractive young woman whom I got to know and like.

The irony of my life at Vilmarhaus was the fact that, as an American citizen, I was technically among the 10% of foreign students admitted there, even though Marburg was my birthplace. I adapted quickly to my new life in the dorm. I now had a small yet attractive room of my own on the first floor which had a small bed, dresser, and desk that faced the window overlooking a pleasant view of a green lawn with trees. I immediately made myself at home by decorating one wall with a tableau of colorful fall leaves that I pasted onto a sheet of cardboard.

Besides the students' rooms, there was also a shared bathroom, a small kitchen with a dining area, and a community room where people could gather to have meetings, parties or other get-togethers. And next to the dorm buildings was a beautiful, spacious community center with a small auditorium called Hans von Soden Haus where meetings, special events, and various performances were held. The neat thing about this building was the upright piano on the second floor that I spent many hours playing.

My new life in the dorm was a far cry from the drab, oppressive, confining environment of the Staatsbibiothek . In fact, as soon as I moved into Vilmarhaus, I switched to working only part-time at the library, so that I could have plenty of time to pursue my studies in *Germanistik* (German Literature) at the nearby Phillipps Universitaet. I was blown away by the incredibly low cost of tuition, compared to what I had to pay in the U.S. For an entire semester of courses, I only had to pay about 60DM (Deutschmarks), which, with the then favorable rate of exchange, amounted to about $20.00. Nor was my dorm room that expensive. In fact, I was now able to pay for tuition, food, and my dorm room with the part-time wages I was earning at the library.

Even though I had already brushed up my knowledge of German with some classes at the nearby *Lessingkolleg* (German language school), I was ill-prepared for university study. At Xavier and Ohio State, all my courses were graded on an A-F basis. I was expected to take regular quizzes, tests, and exams, as well as write a lot of term papers, all of which determined my grade. However, here in Marburg, the university had a pass-fail system. If you passed a course, you were given a *Schein* (certificate of completion), indicating you had successfully completed that class. Furthermore, there were no tests or exams. Your final grade was determined by a group paper in which all the students took part.

Since my written German was still below par, I had a hard time writing my portion of the assigned paper, so needed a lot of help from my classmates to get the job done. There was also something else that turned out to be completely different from my studies in the U.S. Phillipps Universitaet had recently gone Marxist. That meant that a powerful minority of left-leaning students had thrown out many of the old-guard conservative professors, replacing them with younger, Marxist-oriented teachers. In fact, in one of my first classes, *Einfuehrung in die Literaturwissenschaft* (An Introduction to Literature), we were expected to read books by Karl Marx, Friedrich Engels, and modern Marxist writers like Walter Benjamin and Benjamin Adorno. It was hard enough for me to comprehend classic German authors like Goethe, Schiller, and Heine, but I found it next to impossible to wade through the turgid prose of the Marxist writers. Instead of a classroom, we now met in someone's apartment. Fortunately, I was never tested on my comprehension of these texts. The other students did most of the writing for the required *gruppenarbeit* (group term paper) that determined my grade, while I just pitched in as best I could.

Another experience that shook me up happened during one of my seminars. It was a course on the novels of Guenther Grass, who wrote the internationally famous *The Tin Drum* that was later made into a powerful movie. One morning as the young instructor was lecturing on the text of one of Grass's novels, a group of students shouted him down by telling him that what he was teaching was now irrelevant, that they should focus instead on a protest action they were planning that week. The professor was totally intimidated, and I was pretty scared myself. I had heard in American news reports that such things were common in the late '60s on some left-leaning American campuses like Berkeley, Chicago, and Columbia, but I had never experienced anything like this at conservative Xavier or Ohio State.

I also found out that one of the students living next to me in the dorm was an avowed Marxist and DKP (Deutsche Kommunistische Partei) member. One day, he corralled me by trying to convince me of the superiority of the East German government over West Germany's. He told me about the evils of the fascistic government under Nixon, and informed me of the necessity of doing away with the bourgeois Democracy now governing Germany, in favor of a socialist regime. He kept expounding on the virtues of the dictatorshop of the proletariat, in which violence was justified in order to change the current corrupt regime. His views reminded me of the radicalism of Malcolm X.

My life at Vilmarhaus wasn't completely restricted to politics. I soon began to make some friends at the dorm. Since I loved to cook my own meals, I'd often encounter fellow students in the kitchen. Sometimes, when I got brave enough to play my guitar in the community room, some others would join me to listen or play. But since I was pretty shy, I also spent a lot of time in my room playing music or reading. I also struggled with recurring bouts of depression which would sometimes last for weeks or even months. During those times, I'd hole up in my room to spend hours on end strumming my guitar or sleeping, not daring to venture out except to work or attend classes. So, gradually I found myself living in four separate worlds. There was the world of work at Die Staatsbibliothek, my dorm life at Vilmarhaus, my studies at Phillipps Universitaet, and my continued contact with Tante Lucie whom I would visit every couple of weeks.

One of the most significant events of my early months at Vilmarhaus, was getting to know my first close friend. His name was Ebenezer Touleassi and he lived across the hall from me. He was a theology student from Togo, West Africa. We had something in common in that we both loved playing folk songs on the guitar. One song we both loved to sing together was *Swing Low, Sweet Charriot*. I remember how impressed I was when I first visited his room. It was beautifully decorated with multi-colored tapestries which transported me to his African home. Ebenezer had a very attractive, outgoing personality that others in the dorm were also drawn to. Next to him and across the hall from me lived an attractive young woman named Julia who was also very welcoming. She would often invite Ebenezer, me, and other dorm mates for coffee, tea, and pastries.

Then there was another man on my floor whose life would soon intersect with mine in a very significant way. His name was Ottmar. He was, what was called in German, *ein ewiger* student (a perennial student) because he had been enrolled at the university for some eighteen semesters with no end in sight. At that time the rules governing the length of time a student could stay at the university were very lax, and Ottmar took full advantage. When I met him, he had already been working on his doctoral dissertation on the poems of an obscure modern German poet named Georg Trakl for some three or four years.

But what set Ottmar apart from the other students in the dorm was his severe mental illness. He suffered from schizophrenia which caused him to do bizarre things like appearing in the Marburg market square to distribute flowers to strangers, haranguing them about Jesus, or standing in the middle of the street half-naked. In fact, he often thought of himself as a kind of Jesus figure. Ottmar was engaged to a woman some five years older named Annemie who worked as a high school teacher in Koblenz. Although they met regularly, his engagement didn't stop him from avidly pursuing Julia almost to the point of stalking her, serenading her with his poetry. For some reason I still don't rightly understand, Ottmar was attracted to me although I was somewhat wary of him because I was struggling with my own recurring episodes of depression.

One day about six months after I had moved into Vilmarhaus, Ottmar introduced me to Annemie who soon developed a crush on me even though I wasn't that attracted to her physically. Things came to a head in the summer of 1972 when Ottmar invited me to join him, Annemie, her pot-smoking brother Peter, and some friends of theirs on a trip to Denmark. We drove there in two cars. During the trip, Ottmar's mental illness got worse. I often feared for my life while he was at the wheel. He would spend hours expounding on the poetry of Trakl, or talking about his struggles with the demons in his head, or his visions of Jesus. While Ottmar was acting increasingly crazy, Annemie let me know that she was very attracted to me. One night while Ottmar, Annemie, and I were sharing a tent, she encouraged me to make love to her even though Ottmar was sleeping right next to us. So, I climbed into her sleeping bag, where I had my first sexual experience with a woman. I recall getting up the next morning feeling a mixture of exhileration and guilt. Although Ottmar never spoke about this incident, I think he knew what was happening, and his attitude towards me became more guarded, even though he still remained my friend. But I also became more wary of him.

As the months progressed, I got to know more people on my floor at Vilmarhaus. Some of us would often gather for community meals or parties. Sometimes I'd bring out my guitar to play some of my favorite folk songs. Julia and Ebenezer often came to these community gatherings where we'd drink wine or champagne, talk about politics, and catch up on what each others were doing.

I stayed at Vilmarhaus for two years until the winter of 1973 when I had to move out because of the time limit on my stay. During those two years, Ebenezer became my closest friend, as well as an older man named Jochen whom I'd gotten to know at the Staatsbibliothek. I continued studying at Phillipps Universitaet for about a year, after which I transferred to another university in the nearby city of Giessen. I somehow got it into my head that I might find work as an elementary school teacher if I got a degree in elementary education at the Justus Liebig Paedagogische Hochschule (Teachers' College) in Giessen. I remember having to take a long train ride there and back to Marburg to get to and from my classes. But I don't remember much about the classes themselves except that I really didn't know what I wanted, and continued to flounder academically.

While I was staying in Vilmarhaus, I got a job teaching a weekly course in English conversation at the Behringwerke, a language school similar to the Lessingkolleg, but for employees of the Behringwerke, a medical supplies company. However, teaching proved to be quite an ordeal for me since I was pretty shy to begin with, and had never taught before. I remember feeling a rush of anxiety each week before the start of my class. I had a devil of a time knowing how to organize my materials, and ended up using issues of *Newsweek* to teach English conversation. I also dreaded the students' questions about grammar or syntax which I was often unable to answer. Fortunately, my class was pretty small –only about four or five students. And I quit after just one session. I remember the great sense of relief I felt after I quit teaching.

After moving out of Vilmarhaus I was able to find a small room in the private home of someone I'd gotten to know at the university. I stayed there until the spring of 1973 when I decided to move back to the U.S. because I was uncertain about my job prospects in Germany. But before I left Marburg, I had one more very brief and powerful sexual encounter with an American woman named Jackie whom I met at a dance in Hans Von Soden Haus. She was drawn to me because of my fluency in German. I was very attracted to her physically in a way I hadn't been with Annemie who was rather plain. But our liaison turned out to be very short. I soon found out to my dismay that she wasn't really interested in long term relationship, but was just using me to help her hone her German language skills.

During the spring of 1973, I began applying to various American universities which offered Masters degrees in library sciences in hopes of someday becoming a professional librarian. Fortunately, I was accepted by one of these - Case Western Reserve University in Cleveland, Ohio. That meant that I'd be living close enough to my dad, so I could visit him regularly. In June 1973 I moved out of my temporary Marburger digs to return to America where I moved to Cleveland to pursue a Masters in Library Science at Case Western Reserve University.

FINAL ABSOLUTION

When all seems lost in fear and dread,
And hope is hanging by a thread,
The phoenix lifts its fiery head
To raise itself up from the dead.

When fear invades our every pore,
And leaves our souls an open sore,
Our healing breath slips through the door,
And touches us inside our core.

We live inside our aches and pains,
And try so hard to clean the stains
That spread upon our sheets and drain
The hope we need to keep us sane.

We pray unto a God unseen
Upon whom we depend and lean,
Who sheds for us his healing balm,
Restores our stormy hearts to calm.

VII – Final Absolution

I've suffered from recurring bouts of depression and anxiety all of my adult life. I didn't become aware of it being depression until I was an undergraduate at Xavier University. Before that, I just thought there was something seriously wrong with me, that I was defective in some way. However, by the time I started as an undergraduate at Xavier, I realized it was depression. During those times, I found it hard to do my school work or attend classes. I spent a lot of time sleeping or listening to music, and avoided human contact as much as possible.

I recall an especially severe, long-lasting episode at the beginning of my sophomore year. Things got so bad that I thought of killing myself by jumping off a bridge or a high building. In my junior year, while associate editor of the Xavier literary magazine, *The Athenaeum* , I submitted my first poem, *Gas Jet Epitaph*, about a man who commits suicide by turning on the gas. Here is an excerpt from that poem:

GAS JET EPITAPH

Back bent double in the attic seat,
Windows barred and door locked fast,
The note scrawled tritely on the dresser,
Man's half-torn testimony of futility.

Grief multiplies the foolish scribbling,
Record of a witless sigh – an uncompleted sentence
Chokes on itself as noose draws tighter
To twist forth final bluish whisper: "I want…"

Rigor mortis reflected in the upturned whites.
Moist stare at window pane accompanied by
Whine of strings and pounding drum-beat;
Outside, rain drops ashen on the glass – epitaph for darkened room.

Now I realize that these depressive episodes were probably the result of my early abandonment, the loss of my mother at five, and my frequent moves and change of schools. Throughout my life I hardly stayed in one place long enough to establish any roots or firm foundation. My depression was usually triggered by some major loss or change. For example, when I left Marion Hall in my senior year to move back with my dad, I really missed my friend Gene.

Other major triggering events included my girlfriend Pat breaking up with me, losing my graduate fellowship, dropping out of graduate school, and moving back to Cincinnati to work in a factory. But during all these times, I had no idea of how to get help, or even talk about what I was experiencing because of the powerful stigma involved. I always felt a profound sense of shame, and got the message that it was not O.K. to talk about these things.

It wasn't until the fall of 1970 when I had moved back to Germany, that I first sought out help. Things had gotten so bad while working full-time in the dark confines of the Marburger Staatsbibliothek , that I once more thought of committing suicide. I didn't know how to talk about how I was feeling with Tante Lucie or the people I worked with at the library because of the intense shame involved. But fortunately, I finally sought out help from a student counseling center at the university. There I saw a psychologist who first diagnosed me. He told me I suffered from major depression and a *schwacher egoidentitaet* (a weak sense of self). He then suggested I attend a weekly therapy group for students. I began attending this group about the same time I began studying at Phillipps Universitaet, and continued to do so for about a year. Most of the other members were students like myself. They all suffered from some form of depression, but many of them talked as much about politics as their personal feelings.

Since that time in Marburg, I've had frequent recurring episodes of depression and anxiety, sometimes lasting for weeks, sometimes for months on end. After returning home to the U.S. in 1973 to pursue a degree in library science, I had a temporary reprieve because I got so busy with my studies. But as soon I moved to Minnesota in the fall of 1974 to pursue yet another Master's degree, I experienced another severe episode. And in the summer of 1975, while living alone in a small rooming house in Dinkytown, cut off from the previous friends I'd made, and with no job prospects, I fantasized about jumping off the Washington Avenue bridge near the U of M. I had read about a well-known poet and

U of M college professor named John Berryman who had done just that.

But fortunately, I sought out help instead, first at a U of M student counseling center, and later at a place in South Minneapolis called Walk-In Counseling. They in turn referred me to a weekly therapy group at the Government Center facilitated by a clinical social worker. I went there for three years. And since then I've sought out help whenever my mood began to cascade downward. For example, I lived for two and a half years in a residential treatment center for severely mentally ill adults where I had an individual therapist, group therapy, as well as other more unconventional interventions like yoga and bioenergetics.

Not all these programs were helpful, however. I was badly hurt in one unconventional day-treatment program called The Center for Creative Living, which used re-parenting and regression therapy, as well as frequent confrontation and shaming techniques. But for the most part, the day-treatment programs and therapy groups were very helpful. About twenty years ago, I also began seeing a number of psychiatrists and psychiatric nurses who prescribed a great variety of anti-depressants and anti-anxiety medications. One of the most helpful programs was the Fairview Senior Outpatient Program whose therapists were very knowledgeable and sympathetic. Another service I found to be very beneficial was called Adult Rehab Mental Health Services. Thanks to their support, I was able to stay out of the hospital. There I worked with a number of combination therapist/case workers who came to my home once a week to see how I was doing, and help me set weekly goals. Of course, I couldn't have done it without the help of several fine individual therapists who not only helped me work through my early abandonment issues, sense of up-rootedness, and low self esteem, but also encouraged me to express myself creatively through music, writing, and storytelling.

Besides seeking out help, I've also become a mental health advocate through NAMI (the National Alliance on Mental Illness) by talking about my recovery journey through their In Our Own Voice program.

I've found other ways besides therapy to decrease my depressive episodes and periods of anxiety. One of the most important is my faith community where I'm a part of many support groups and have made some of my closest friends. Doing various forms of exercise at the Y like yoga, T'ai Chi, aerobics, and swimming also helps a lot, as well as riding my bike, taking walks, and jogging. Expressing myself creatively through music, writing, and storytelling also goes a long way towards maintaining my mental health. Yes, I feel best when I'm playing music on my autoharp, composing songs, and writing in my journal.

Right now, thanks to an excellent therapist who works with other adoptees, my church friends, medications, regular exercise, and creative expression, I've been depression-free for the past nine months, and hope to remain so for a long time to come.

AUTOHARP FOR CHRISTMAS

I want an autoharp for Christmas,
So I can strum my blues away.
I want to hear them old-time ballads
That Mother Maybelle used to play,
And wile away the winter hours
With Yuletide carols warm and bright,
Like Jingle Bells and Hark the Herald,
What Child is This and Silent Night.

I want an autoharp for Christmas,
Just give me any model please,
Chromatic or diatonic,
So I can pick those melodies.
I'll play my heart out on three octaves,
My fingers dancing o'er the strings,
And then I'll tune up for the New Year
To find out what tomorrow brings.

VIII – From Love to Addiction

My love affair with the autoharp began in the winter of 1976. At that time, I was living in a small rooming house near the U of M campus with seven other students whom I'd met a year before at an international residence called Namche House. I had just quit the English as a Second Language

Master's Degree program, and was working as a stock clerk at Sears on Chicago and Lake. But I spent most of my spare time listening to folk music, or playing my guitar and harmonica. I checked out a lot of folk and rock records from the downtown Minneapolis library. Some of my favorite recording artists at the time included Bob Dylan, Judy Collins, Doc Watson, Simon and Garfunkel, John Denver, and Tom Paxton.

However, one day I discovered an unusual-looking old album entitled *Mountain Music Played on the Autoharp*. The front cover depicted several fancy, antique-looking autoharps. On the back were pictures of three old men playing the autoharp. I'd never heard of any of them before – Pop Stoneman, Neriah Benfield, and Kilby Snow. The liner notes mentioned that their recordings were made in the thirties and forties. Up to that time I'd never heard of an autoharp, nor seen one played. I checked out the album and brought it home. It immediately became my favorite even though I had never heard that kind of music before. When I played it over and over again on my one-speaker stereo player, I noticed that one of the musicians- Kilby Snow - accompanied his autoharp with a harmonica which he held in a holder. At this time, I was already playing guitar and harmonica a la Dylan.

I immediately fell in love with this old-time music which evoked the mountain hollers in Kentucky, West Virginia, and North Carolina. The picking was fast and furious and the singing full of rich harmonies. I kept renewing the album from the library until I knew every tune by heart.

During the next three years, I experienced a series of synchronistic events that opened up the world of the autoharp for me in ways I could not have foreseen. In spring of 1977, I attended an arts and crafts camp for adults called Northlands Rec Lab, located at a YMCA camp near Hudson, Wisconsin. Our song leader, Jan, played the autoharp to accompany the songs we sang after breakfast each morning. She got me started by showing me a few basic strums and chord progressions. Two years later, in the spring of 1979, I attended Rec Lab again. This time our song leader, Beth, was a very vivacious, charismatic woman who also accompanied her singing with the autoharp, but played it in a more dynamic way that really got me excited. She was very friendly and showed me new ways of playing the instrument.

About a week later, I had a chance to volunteer for a Minnesota folk music festival in the Cedar Riverside area in Minneapolis. During one of the evening concerts, I heard a wonderfully versatile folk musician from the East Coast named Bob Zentz who played the autoharp in a way I'd never heard before. He not only used it to accompany his singing, but he also played melodies on it. He was equally proficient in about half a dozen other instruments as well, such as fiddle, guitar, hammered dulcimer, and harmonica. I was green with envy.

During the festival, I attended my first autoharp workshop, hosted by an attractive diminutive woman named Stevie Beck. I loved the way she played her autoharp solos – Appalachian ballads, fiddle tunes, slip jigs, and old cowboy songs. During her workshop, she casually mentioned that she taught autoharp at her home. So, I started taking private lessons from her that summer. She turned out to be the best music teacher I ever had, and taught me all the basic autoharp techniques – the pinch-thumb strum, the hammer-on, melody picking, and her famous autoharp playing technqiue called "schling." At this time Stevie was also working as a luthier in a nearby guitar shop, fixing autoharps and guitars. In fact, she helped me pick out my very first autoharp.

I always looked forward to my lessons with Stevie. Each week, she'd write out new song arrangements in TAB, a kind of instrument specific musical notation without sheet music, and record them on tape. She also loved to tell stories. One time she told me how she was involved with this new live radio show in St. Paul called *The Prairie Home Companion Show* hosted by Garrison Keillor. It turned out that she taught Garrison how to play the autoharp. He later returned the favor by billing her as the Queen of the Autoharp on his show. I took lessons from Stevie for about six months. After that, I was ready to venture out on my own. I played the autoharp every chance I got.

While taking lessons from Stevie, I was working at a North Minneapolis nursing home called Oak Ridge Care Center. There I led various musical programs for the residents, either playing for groups in the dayroom, or serenading individual residents in their rooms. It was the first job I'd had where I was able to use my music. When I started there, I played mostly guitar and harmonica. But I quickly discovered that the folk songs I was used to playing didn't make much of an impact on the residents, most of whom were in their seventies, eighties, and nineties. They just couldn't relate to songs like Bob Dylan's *Blowin' in the Wind*, Leonard Cohen's *Bird on the Wire*, or Paul Simon's *Sounds of Silence*. So, I quickly learned to expand my musical horizons by going back to the library to borrow all the *Sing Along With Mitch* albums I could get my hands on, and learning songs like *Five Foot Two, Let Me Call You Sweetheart*, and *You Are My Sunshine*. I soon discovered that the autoharp was ideally suited to accompanying the songs seniors liked, especially those old gospel songs and hymns they loved so much.

Two years later, in the spring of 1981, I got my first chance to teach an autoharp class at a community ed program in Minneapolis. One of my four students became a good friend who later began teaching autoharp herself. And about a year later, in the summer of 1982, another unique opportunity came my way when I saw a small ad in the Help Wanted section of *The Minneapolis Tribune* that said simply: "Autoharp teacher wanted at the West Bank School of Music." I couldn't believe my luck! I'd been taking guitar and banjo classes there for years, yet I never dreamed I would eventually be teaching there. If ever there was job made for me, this was it! I auditioned and got the position. So, now I found myself teaching autoharp at the West Bank School of Music! I found out later that Stevie Beck had taught there before me.

As the years went by, I had many neat experiences in connection with the autoharp. I began subscribing to a wacky, yet wonderful magazine called *The Autoharpoholic* which contained song and instrumental arrangements of autoharpists from all over the country and the world. It also included funny commentaries and listings of upcoming folk music festivals. Unfortunately, *The Autohapaholic* stopped publication after ten years. Yet I was able to publish my very first autoharp arrangement in it, a Scandinavian tune called *Helsa dem der Hemma*, before that happened.

After *The Autoharpoholic* ceased publication, I found out about another autoharp magazine called *Autoharp Clearinghouse*. This time I got to know the editor in a more personal way. I sent her some more of my autoharp arrangements, a good number of which she published. It turned out that we had a special connection – our mutual German heritage. So, I sent her several German Christmas carols I'd learned as a boy. And, lo and behold, she published all of them! It was a big thrill when she also reviewed my first studio tape of original songs for autoharp and guitar. A few years later she did a cover profile of me in the March 1998 issue. Unfortunately, *Autoharp Clearinghouse* also ceased publication a few years later.

In the course of the next few years, I gradually, lost my autoharp connections as things took a turn for the worse autoharpically speaking. For one thing, more and more music stores stopped selling autoharps or harp accessories. For another, my Community Ed students dwindled down to nothing. But the worst blow was losing my autoharp teaching job at the West Bank School of Music.

However, my love affair with the autoharp was far from over. Over the next few years I discovered two new music festivals which both held autoharp contests, one in Winfield, Kansas called Walnut Valley Bluegrass Festival , and another near Harrisburg Pennsylvania called Mountain Laurel Autoharp Gathering. Both of these featured autoharp contests in which I participated, yet never made it to the finals. I also enjoyed attending their concerts and workshops. In the past thirty years, I've also recorded ten cassette tapes/CDs featuring the autoharp and my original songs. Until COVID-19, I also played the autoharp every week for our Sunday church service.

And in 2005, in order to meet other autoharp players, I founded a local club for autoharp players called Twin Cities Autoharpers who met monthly to jam, share songs, and plan concerts. Through this group I got to make several good friends. Even though I discontinued facilitating it several years ago, I still continue to play the autoharp every chance I get. As a matter of fact, I recently made a CD featuring classical and popular instrumentals for autoharp called *Classical Autoharp in Ragtime*.

FREE YOUR MUSICAL SPIRIT

Free your musical spirit,
Free your musical soul,
Sing it out loud to the rafters,
Sing it out loud and bold.

There's times when I feel like crying,
There's times when I'm sad and blue,
There's always something a-dying,
But there's always something new.

Music brings joy to the lonely,
Puts a smile on the saddest face,
There's a song inside every person,
And each song has its time and place.

So, don't go hide in your cellars,
Don't bury your face in the ground,,
Stand up and look at the sunshine,
And let the music resound!

IX – Adventures in Recording

In the past thirty years, I've recorded three tapes and eight CDs of original songs and instrumental arrangements for the autoharp. I also recorded two CDs featuring musical highlights from the Walker Open Stage which I hosted monthly for some twenty years from 1988 to 2008. During this time, I've worked with six different recording engineers.

I'll never forget the time and place of my very first recording session at Walker United Methodist Church on Sunday May 20, 1990. I recorded mostly my own songs with the help of a man with the distinctive name of Armand French. I met him while playing Jesu Man's *Joy of Desiring* at a Walker wedding a few months before. When he asked me if I ever considered making my own recording, I was hesitant at first because I didn't know what that would entail, or how much it would cost. But he persuaded me to do so. I remember how nervous I was because I had never done anything like that before. But Armand not only made me feel comfortable, but also gave me a good deal.

On the appointed day, he set up the speakers, monitors, mikes, and other sound equipment. I proceeded to do a live concert with my best friend George Staupe and a couple of other musician friends. My first recording was a cassette tape entitled *Free Your Musical Spirit*, named after a song I'd written a few years before. That song was inspired by a campaign conducted by the West Bank School of Music where I was teaching autoharp at the time. Their slogan ran: "Free your musical spirit, sign up for lessons at the WBSM."

A few years later I recorded my second tape with Armand, once more at a live concert at Walker Church. Called *Gifts of Nature*, it contained all original songs. Around this time I also got to know a talented guitarist-singer-songwriter named Layah who invited me to record some harmonica tracks on her demo of original songs. She introduced me to the man who recorded her demo whose name was Mark. Mark had an elaborate 16-track recording studio in his basement, as well as some high-end mikes and other sound equipment.

It was there that I embarked upon my first studio recording which I named after my new song *Atom Bomb Baby*. It took me almost a year to make this recording because I was struggling with recurring depression at the time. It turned out to be the most ambitious project I'd embarked on thus far. Mark encouraged me to record multiple tracks. So, I invited several friends like George, Brad, and John to lay down additional tracks to enhance the total effect. In the end, this tape featured not only my autoharp, guitar, and harmonica, but also Brad's accordion, George's dobro, and John's guitar.

I was very impressed with Mark's elaborate studio which he had painstakingly built up over the years. He would often regale me with stories about how he acquired his recording equipment, or worked with various musicians and bands. This time, I really enjoyed the recording process. It was very exciting to see what effects I could add to my songs that I couldn't have done in a live recording.

It is neat how often significant life events are linked together. While working on my Atom Bomb Baby recording, my friend John also expressed an interest in recording a CD of his own with Mark. This led to my next recording project and my first CD. John had built up his own recording studio at his home and offered to record my first CD free of charge. It was called *I Remember*, contained all original songs, and was recorded soon after 911. In fact, the title cut, *I Remember*, refers to that tragedy. With John, the recording process was much more informal since he was a friend. He laid down some additional tracks on his guitar, dobro, and synthesizer. I even invited the Walker Singers to sing on the chorus of one of my songs.

Around this time, I was becoming friends with a very talented singer/ drummer at Walker Church named Mary who often sang with me at various Walker events. So, in 2007 I invited her to sing with me on my next CD of original songs called *Yin of my Yang*. I named this CD after the Yin Yang symbol we used on the church altar. By this time, I had also met another recording engineer named Amy, who had built a state-of-the-art recording studio in her basement. Amy, who was very friendly and supportive, made both Mary and me feel very comfortable in her studio. She made the recording process fun, exciting, and enjoyable. Besides *Yin of my Yang*, I also made two other CDs with Mary and Amy, as well as an instrumental autoharp CD called *Classical Autoharp in Ragtime* which featured classical and ragtime tunes.

It was with Amy, that Mary and I also began recording my next CD, *Pandora*, but for reasons I still don't quite understand, Amy dropped out of my life at this time. So, I completed this CD with yet another recording person I met at Walker named Jim. Although his home was in Chisago City, about 35 miles notheast of Minneapolis, Mary was able to give me rides there. Jim too had turned one of his rooms into a makeshift recording studio. But both Mary and I really missed working with Amy.

And that brings me to my most recent recording and my sixth recording person. This recording, called *Eerodynamic!*, is named after Mary's then two-year-old grandson, Eero, whom I got to know from infancy. It contains all original children's songs, most of which I sing with Mary who also accompanies me on the drum. This time I found yet another recording engineer named Bruce who also did a recording of our Walker Church pick-up band. Like Mark, John, Amy and Jim, Bruce also had his own recording studio set up at his home. We hit it off immediately and both Mary and I really enjoyed working with him.

Making these recordings with the various engineers I've worked with over the past thirty years, has been quite a thrilling adventure. The recording process itself has become increasingly enjoyable and boosted my confidence. In fact, as of the publication of this memoir, I've recorded another CD of original songs with Bruce called *Unicorns & Rainbows*.

A STORY

A story is worth more than a thousand words
It transports you to a land
Where anything is possible.
It visits you in your dreams and waking fantasies,
And sustains you through your darkest nights.

A story was what our ancestors first told
When they discovered language.
Back when they painted their cave walls
With animals and hunts,
The storyteller brought them close,
Fired their imaginations,
And protected them from their fears.

A story is what opened up a new world for me,
A world of caring tellers who encouraged me to tell,
And brought me healing for an aching soul
That had lost its way.

X – Born into Stories

I've lived in Minneapolis since 1974. I came here in the spring of 1974 to enroll in an English as a Second Language graduate program at the U of M. At the time, I was hoping to teach English in Japan or Europe after I had graduated. But life had its own agenda for me, and I dropped out of school after only one quarter. However, I liked Minnesota so much that I decided to make Minneapolis my permanent home.

In 1983, I got involved in some creative writing groups. Although I had kept a journal since my sophomore year in college, I remained pretty much of a closet writer. But now I felt ready to expand my horizons. So, I enrolled in an extensive creative writing program at Whittier Park in South Minneapolis where I took classes in journal writing, poetry, and playwriting. There, I met lots of talented people who were on a similar creative path.

Joining the Whittier Writers' Workshop was very important for me because I had always felt inadequate about my writing ability. Even though my college major was English, and my dad an English professor (maybe *because* of that), I wasn't able to find my own writing voice. Nor was I confident enough to submit my own poems and short stories for publication, or to share them in public. So, I was very happy to explore this new opportunity to do more creative writing.

One day in the middle of January 1983, a student from one of my writing classes told me about this storytelling group that met at Whittier park once a month on Sunday nights in their Fireside Room. This was a cozy little nook with a small sofa, some armchairs, and a semi-circular fireplace which was put to good use during those bone-chilling Minnesota winter nights. So, one evening in January, I decided to check it out.

At this point in my life, I knew next to nothing about storytelling. I still believed the myth that storytelling was primarily for kids. I knew that people told folk and fairy tales to kids in schools and libraries. In fact, before I moved to Minnesota, I had planned to become a librarian myself, having just completed my MLS degree at Case Western Reserve University in Cleveland. I was looking for a library position in the Twin Cities while attending grad school at the U of M. But I wasn't sure what kind of library work I wanted to do.

Being a children's librarian sounded vaguely intriguing until I found out that one of their main responsibilities was telling stories to kids. When I heard that, I quickly lost interest. I'd never told a story to anyone before, much less kids. And the thought of facing a bunch of restless, fidgety three and four year olds with fifteen-second attention spans terrified the day lights out of me. So, I decided instead to apply for a safer job like reference librarian at a public library. But, as things turned out, life again had its own agenda for me, and I wasn't able to secure any library

job anywhere because of the 1974 recession which hit just after I had graduated from library school.

Which brings me back to that first storytelling group at Whittier Park. I got there having no idea of what to expect. I certainly couldn't imagine myself telling stories to anyone, not even adults. While growing up, my dad was always the storyteller. And he was a natural. At parties he'd often talk for hours, describing his life in Germany (where both of us were born), his student and teaching days at the University of Cincinnati and Xavier, or his extensive travels in Europe. In the meantime, his former students and professor friends would gather around to listen intently. I always envied him because he was in the limelight, whereas I stayed in the shadows, shy, unobtrusive, and taciturn, especially in groups. I hardly ever said anything, but just listened, always listened. And, by the time I did get in a few words, I was usually interrupted. So, I didn't know what to expect from this Whittier group. I saw a mixed group of about seven or eight tellers. They went around the circle, each one taking turns to tell a story while the others listened intently. When each one had finished telling, the others gave him or her feedback, followed by an animated discussion about storytelling.

As the tales unfolded, I gradually warmed to the blazing fire in front of me, and became more comfortable. I noticed how respectfully people listened to each other. There were no interruptions or cross-talk. I'd never seen that before, and was very impressed. I recall one attractive woman in her thirties who wore a beautiful white, fairy god-mother costume and told a tale about the spirit of Whittier Park which was celebrating its 100th anniversary that year. On her head she wore a tiara, and in one hand she waved a magic wand. Her mesmerizing tale made me feel like a little kid again.

Another teller, a man this time, told us about this new political party he had started called the OGP (Old Garden Party). He spoke of communicating with gophers through pipes in the house and back yard, of his boyhood in Bloomington when most of it was still farmland, of the days before his family got a TV, and of the wild escapades of his older cousin Johnny Johnson. Then he got up, grabbed a short piece of garden hose from his bag, and started swinging one end wildly around his head, while playing a tune on the other end with a trumpet mouthpiece. I'd never seen anything like that before! Nor had I ever laughed so hard! It was a real cathartic experience!

As the other tellers regaled us with their tales, I got more and more drawn into their worlds. There was the woman who told the Bible story about Jesus and the woman at the well, which made me feel as if she had been there, and had become that Samaritan woman with her five husbands. One man told a gothic urban legend about a hitch-hiker who kept re-appearing mysteriously.

I don't remember all the stories that night, but I do remember their effect on me. While listening, I felt a powerful kind of healing taking place inside of me which I had never experienced before. It was the kind of healing born of laughter, tears, exuberance, and mystery. By the time I left, I knew that something important had changed inside of me. I still couldn't put my fingers on it, but I knew I wanted more. It couldn't have come at a better time because I had been feeling lonely and adrift After the stories had ended, and I was about to leave, one of the tellers invited me to come back again next month.

So, come back I did. As I became a regular, I gradually got to know some of the other storytellers. I found out the group called itself Storyfront and had started meeting about five years before.

It was not the first time I was involved in an arts group since I was already playing and teaching folk music, attending Open Stages, and involved in the Whittier Writers' Group. But none of those other groups extended me the kind of support I got here. The strange irony in all this was that I'd never dreamed of becoming a storyteller before. But those Storyfronters kept encouraging me to tell whether or not I had any previous experience.

I remember that, after one Sunday evening get-together, one of the tellers invited me to attend a weekend storytelling conference in a small town in Wisconsin called Mineral Point. He was driving there with his wife who was also a teller, and they both offered me a ride. It was quite a thrill, but also very scary since I didn't know a soul except them, and I had no idea of what to expect. At this point I don't think I had even told a story at Storyfront.

But go I did! The conference proved to be quite overwhelming in a good kind of way since I had nothing to compare it with. Around a hundred storytellers from all over the Midwest gathered at a school, where I slept overnight on one of the classroom floors. During the day on Saturday and Sunday, there were storytelling workshops. Friday night, there were ghost stories in an old mansion, and on Saturday night a big storytelling concert featuring about six tellers.

At that point in my life I thought concerts only meant music! I was about to learn differently. I don't recall many specifics about that weekend, except going out to a bar after the Saturday concert. With a few beers in them, some of the guys got pretty rowdy, and so did the tales they told. I vaguely remember one Irishman jumping up on the bar counter to belt out some hilarious, bawdy tales while the others cheered him on.

However, the most memorable event of that weekend took place during the Saturday night concert. One of the featured tellers was a tall, imposing Amish man with a black, broad-brimmed hat and a full beard. He really looked the part with his sturdy farmer build, deep voice, and stern piercing eyes. He told a story about how his wife was murdered in a freak incident. While he spoke, he began to cry while is voice got all choked up with emotion. It seemed as if he were reliving that traumatic nightmare right then and there. For a moment, I was afraid he might fall apart right in front of us. But he managed to pull himself together. After he had finished, he told the audience, most of whom he knew, that this was the first time he had ever shared this story with anyone. For a moment there was stunned silence, followed by thunderous applause that lasted a long time. I too was very moved though I'd never met this man before. It was an experience I would never forget!

After attending the Wisconsin storytelling conference, I began to feel more at ease with the other Storyfront tellers. They continued encouraging me to tell my own stories until one evening I finally got up enough guts to do so. I don't remember what my story was, but I do remember their reaction. For the first time in my life, I felt really listened to. There were no interruptions. And afterwards, I got lots of positive, constructive feedback. Plus, they strongly encouraged me to tell again. It was a real break-through for me, as well as an enormous boost to my confidence. As you can imagine, I didn't get much sleep that night as I replayed that night in my head.

Gradually, I began to tell more often. About a year later, Storyfront moved to another location, a Lutheran church on Franklin Avenue. But we continued to meet on Sunday nights once a month. The only thing I missed was that cozy little fireplace. I also took some storytelling classes, including one from the husband-and-wife team who gave me a ride to that Wisconsin conference. For a while, I even did a brief stint hosting Storyfront evenings after the previous host decided to quit. And a couple of years after that, a vegetarian restaurant near the church called Seward Café began hosting weekly storytelling evenings on Friday nights. Each week, there would be a different theme with a different host who would invite other tellers to join him or her. I soon got involved with this Seward storytelling group, first as a listener, then as a teller, and finally as a host. I remember the first story I told there that was a big hit. It was about the time I won the Bob Dylan Soundalike contest at the 400 Bar in Minneapolis in 1993. This momentous occasion was subsequently shown on a Twin Cities Public TV station in a program called *Only in Minnesota*, narrated by comedian Louie Anderson.

It was also exciting for me to be a storytelling host at Seward Cafe, to invite others to tell with me, and to see my name in their quarterly storytelling calendar. I felt like an explorer discovering new territories. I had never experienced this kind of support from my peers before. As a result, I gradually took myself more seriously as a storyteller, and got to know the other tellers better. The best part was meeting mentors along the way who kept encouraging me by inviting me to participate in their workshops and attend their concerts. I also continued taking storytelling classes while attending annual Northlands Storytelling Network conferences, now relocated to a small town in Northeastern Iowa called Elkader.

Finally, in the summer of 1994, eleven years after attending my first Storyfront meeting at Whittier Park, I would experience my biggest break-through yet. Once more, life was about to have its own agenda for me.

As well as hosting some weekly storytelling nights at Seward Café, I also attended regular meetings to determine who would be the hosts for each three month period. These meetings were conducted by a storytelling calendar coordinator. It was their job to recruit tellers and hosts, as well as put out a quarterly storytelling calendar. When I attended one of those meetings, I found out that the previous coordinator had decided to quit. Since no one else volunteered to do the job, I decided to take the plunge. This was quite a big step for me! Even though the other tellers at the meeting were sure I could handle this new responsibility, I wasn't so sure myself. I was pretty shy about recruiting other tellers, organizing hosts, and dealing with some of the big egos I might encounter. But something inside me told me I could do this. It would be another major step in boosting my self-confidence and taking on a leadership position.

So, for the next two years, I got out the quarterly Seward storytelling calendar, organized meetings, recruited tellers, and made sure there were hosts at the Seward Café each Friday night. Not that there weren't some big challenges along the way, what with the continuing struggles with the café staff, loud kitchen background noises, and money problems. But for the most part, coordinating the Seward calendar turned out to be a great learning experience. And I got lots of positive support and affirmations along the way. In many ways, I felt as if I had come of age. It seemed amazing that in eleven short years, I had gone from timid listener, knowing next to nothing about storytelling, to storytelling host, to coordinator of the quarterly Seward Café storytelling calendar.

Unfortunately, Seward closed its doors to those weekly storytelling evenings after a ten year run. But I soon found other ways to continue telling. A few years after the Seward group ended, I found another storytelling venue. It was called SALT, for Salt of the Earth Storytellers, and met once a month at Central Lutheran Church. The stories in this group focused on spiritual themes. One of the members was a professional storyteller who made her living telling stories in churches, libraries, and women's groups. Some of its members have become good friends.

Over the years, my confidence in telling stories has grown a lot, thanks to those early beginnings when I was supported and encouraged. Now, I often weave music into the stories I tell. I hope to keep on telling and listening for many years to come.

KIRBY PUCKETT- KING OF THE TWINS' OUTFIELD

He was born in the projects on Chicago's Southside,
Of parents who were poor, but had a lot of pride,
He learned to play baseball with a ten-cent rubber ball,
And soon became the Twin we loved the best of all.
He started with the Twins in the year of '84,
Got four hits his first game, wore Number "34,"
Though he was short and squat, he had a mighty swing,
One crack of his bat made that Metrodome ring!

His stats were stupendous, and he had few peers,
No Twin 's player had more hits in his first ten years,
His life-time batting average was a sizzling "318,"
The finest center fielder Minnesota's ever seen!
He made the All-Star team from '86 to '95,
Won six "Golden Gloves," kept the Twins' hopes alive,
He helped them win two series in '87, '91,
With a death-defying catch and a winning home run!

He had to quit the game 'cause of problems with his eyes,
But he made the Hall of Fame on his very first try,
He was a great team player that set him apart,
A Minnesota legend at the old ballpark.
He set a great example 'til the day he died,
A real inspiration and a classy guy,
Both the kids and grown-ups sought his autograph,
And they won't forget his smile and big hearty laugh.
Kirby, Kirby Puckett, King of the Twin's outfield!

XI – Baseball and Me

I really love baseball! It's my favorite big-league sport by far. One of my main ways of relaxing is to listen to Twins' games on the radio. I love to hear the crack of the bat as the ball hits its sweet spot and flies out over the fence for a home run. I love the leisurely pace of the game, as well as those dramatic spurts of excitement when there's a hit-and-run, a stolen base, a pitch out, or a fly ball caught on the warning track. At times I can even be in the mood for a low-scoring pitcher's duel with its multiple strikeouts and dizzying array of pitches. I once heard baseball described as "ritualized boredom" which is not far from the truth, but it misses the magic this game holds for fans like me.

Just the other day, while browsing for some materials on baseball at the Hennepin County Library, I couldn't help but notice how many books have been written on the subject -- shelf after shelf -- much more than any other big league sport like football, hockey, basketball, or golf. It made me wonder why baseball has always held such an appeal for writers. And it seems fitting since they both seem to be intertwined.

Even though I'm not a baseball geek who can quote you tons of statistics about hitters' batting averages or pitchers' ERAs, I do find myself turning to the *Minneapolis StarTribune* sports pages almost daily, now that the Twins are doing so well. I can tell you that Joe Mauer is playing first base, Brian Dozier is hitting in the lead-off spot, and that Glen Perkins is leading the American League with 21 saves (as of June 7, 2015). Of course I shared the excitement of all Twins' fans during their spectacular, World Series winning seasons of 1987 and 1991. I remember getting chills up and down my spine while riding a bus during the 6th game of the 1991 World Series. The bus driver had his radio on so that all his passengers could listen to the play-by-play. I remember how everyone cheered as Kirby Puckett made that spectacular catch in the outfield to rob Atlanta of a potential run, and later hit the home run that sparked the team to victory. I certainly have my baseball heroes: men like Puckett, Rod Carew, Lou Gehrig, Jackie Robinson, and Hank Aaron.

There is a certain mystique about the numbers that baseball players wear on their backs. I think almost every fan knows that Babe Ruth wore Number 3. Number 44 was worn by Hank Aaron whose 715 home runs eclipsed the Babe's record. Number 42 was worn by Jackie Robinson, the first black player on a major league team. It was recently retired so that no other player could ever wear that number again. I think, however, that all the Dodgers wear a Number 42 on Opening Day.

And of course, each team retires the numbers of its most illustrious players once they have finished playing there. My favorite number is 34, worn by Twins' former center fielder: Kirby Puckett. I even wrote a song in his honor which I sent to the Twins' front office during their 1991 season. It's called *Kirby Puckett, King of the Twins' Outfield* and is sung to the tune of *Davy Crockett, King of the Wild Frontier.*

Before becoming a Twins' fan, I followed the Cincinnati Reds in the late 1960s and early '70s during their Big Red Machine days of Pete Rose, Johnny Bench, and Dave Conception. At that time I was working as a copy boy for the Cincinnati Enquirer and would pick up the paper each night after work to scour the sports pages, check the box scores, and see how the Reds were doing.

It was in Cincinnati where my interest in baseball was born when I moved there from Germany at the age of nine. When I was eleven, my dad placed me temporarily with a large Catholic foster family named the Harkins. Their oldest son Patrick, who was twelve at the time, befriended me and showed me the fundamentals of hitting and fielding. He also invited me to join his pals in their after school, backyard games. A few years later, when I was about 15, a Catholic nun named Sister Mary Elissa invited me to join her 8th grade class in Covington, Kentucky for a week. There one of her pupils befriended me and invited me to join him and his friends when they played pick-up games during recess and after school. I was surprised that I could still hold my own with the other kids even though I had hardly ever played since my time with Patrick at the Harkins'.

Many years later when I was in my 40s, I finally got a chance to play on two real teams. Except it wasn't baseball but softball. The first team, called The Companions, was made up of players who all had a mental illness. I got a chance to wear their blue monogrammed uniform shirt and play during one summer. A few years later I joined another softball team called The Minnehaha Mariners which belonged to a mental health drop-in center that I was a member of at the time. Our team was part of a Minneapolis Parks and Recreation League, and we spent the summer playing other drop-in center teams at various city parks.

Initially, the Mariners' coach had me play first base, but when I had a lot of trouble fielding grounders and taking throws from the other bases and the outfield, they put me in right field where I didn't get as many balls hit to me. Despite my less than stellar fielding, I had much better luck hitting the ball and became a consistent singles hitter. And because of my speed, I was usually able to get on base. Fortunately, I was never seriously injured while playing even though I had some close calls. One time, while rounding the bases, a batted ball hit me squarely in the back. Apart from minor bruising, I sustained no damage.

The only time I could have been seriously injured in a game was in the summer of 1969 while I was attending Ohio State and playing a pick-up softball game with my friends Don, John and Elliott. I remember I was pitching while Don was at bat. At one point, he hit a sharp bouncer that smacked me right in the nose. My nose swelled up so much that my friends had to help me home to recuperate. But fortunately, nothing was broken, only my pride.

What I remember most about that summer with The Mariners was not our team's win-loss record, although we did pretty well on that account, winning most of our games. No, what I remember most was the sheer excitement of being part of a real team for the second time in my life. It was neat to experience the camaraderie of my teammates and to share the excitement of winning a close game. It was a big thrill to feel the adrenaline rush as I stood in the batter's box waiting for a pitch I could hit past second base, or the pounding of my heart when I caught my first fly ball in the outfield. Yes, baseball and softball have both given me many happy memories as a fan and a player.

A Walker Welcome

These people have blessed me and made me feel welcome,
Encouraged my spirit to enter and dwell with them,
Opened their arms, asked me into their circle,
Opened their hearts into their loving family. Yes!

Shalom was the word to describe the peace they sought,
Following the way of truth, what Jesus taught. Yes! Yes! Yes!
Shalom was the word to describe the peace they sought,
Following the way of truth, what Jesus taught. Yes! Yes! Yes!

It wasn't denominal doctrines that drew me in,
Or turnstile of pastors that made my head spin,
But general fellowship I sensed was felt by all,
Caused me to join them, got me to heed their call. Yes! Yes! Yes!

XII – Amazing Grace

In August 1986, a friend named Shelley encouraged me to attend a church in South Minneapolis that I had heard a lot about – Walker United Methodist Church. In the summer of 1980, I had volunteered there at a community radio station called KFAI, located in a small space on the third floor. But I had never attended a Walker church service. However, that was to change on that sunny day in August when I went there with Shelley to attend a service in Powderhorn Park. I was surprised to find out I already knew the presiding minister from another lifetime. Roger had been the director of Wellspring, the residential treatment program I had attended from 1979 to 1981.

Roger recognized me too, welcomed me, encouraged me to come back, and suggested I bring along my autoharp so I could join the musicians who played at the beginning of each service. So, come back I did. On my next visit, I met the main minister, Bryan Peterson, who, I later found out, had been minister at Walker since 1967 when he completely transformed the previous worship service.

It was fortunate that I found Walker Church at this time since I was going through a particularly difficult time in my life. I had just quit an abusive day-treatment program in West St. Paul that had not only left me traumatized, but also caused me to lose my entire support community. It was also good that I found a spiritual community since I had stopped attending church a long time before because of my differences with the Catholic religion I grew up with.

I immediately felt welcomed at Walker. The next time I came, I brought along my autoharp and harmonica to join their weekly pick-up band that played each Sunday before the service. From the very beginning, Bryan encouraged me to become a member. Although hesitant at first, I finally joined in December of that year. I soon got involved in a lot of Walker activities like the Walker Singers and the membership committee. Eventually, I even taught a journal writing class in their adult education program. That winter, Walker celebrated the hundred year anniversary of its founding.

With the encouragement of Bryan, I also began hosting a monthly Open Stage night in the fall of 1988 which I continued for twenty years. I knew I was in the right place when Bryan preached a sermon one Sunday on the subject of spiritual abuse. I liked the fact that people at Walker welcomed all forms of faith expression including Wicca and Buddhism. In fact, each service included a reading from the Tao by Lao Tse. They also welcomed GBLTQ members. I soon began to make quite a few new friends there.

Things continued to go well until the summer of 1989 when Bryan died of a sudden heart attack. He was only 51 years old. I was out of the country at the time, visiting friends in Germany, but I heard later that they had a huge turnout at the memorial service to honor Byan's many contributions to the community. For about six months we had a transitional minister. Then a new young woman minister named Pamela was hired. I liked her right away because she was a gentle, kind soul who had lots of fresh ideas. I remember one big planning meeting at the beautiful home of two members who lived in Jordan, Minnesota. We mapped out future goals and charted our new direction after Bryan's death. Pamela also had a special gift of attracting new members.

Unfortunately, Pamela quit being a minister after only two years in order to devote more time to her two young children. A new, more conservative minister named Judy was hired to take her place. Although Judy tried her best to fit into the Walker community which was pretty set in its own way, she wasn't welcomed by some of the powers that be, and was asked to leave after only two years. That sent Walker spiraling downward into another crisis. Fortunately, however, the church community recovered when they hired Roger, the former associate minister, to become their new full-time minister.

Roger stayed for nine years during which time the Walker community grew and thrived. I really liked his impassioned Sunday sermons which were not only intellectually stimulating, but also drawn from Roger's personal experiences. Roger was also very active in the men's group and various social justice activities. He facilitated a spiritual life group I attended which included mindfulness meditation and personal sharing. Although I never really got close to Roger personally, I liked how he was able to bring our community together.

After Roger retired, a new minister named Seth was hired to take his place. Seth was a very talented musician and dedicated minister. He had a special gift for relating to kids. Unfortunately, he suffered from severe depression which often got in the way of his being more effective. One Sunday in July, shortly after his father, who was also a minister, commented negatively on one of his sermons, Seth committed suicide. That sent the whole community into another crisis of faith. Fortunately, the Methodist hierarchy hired an interim retired minister named Larry to help us through the painful transition. After Seth's death, Larry convened an all-church meeting where Walker members were able to share their grief, as well as chart out a direction for the future. Larry stayed for a year after which a new minister named Walter was hired on a part-time basis.

Walter was our minister for some thirteen years, longer than anyone except Bryan himself. He was a strong advocate for the GBLTQ community and very active in the annual Gay Pride Parade. He was a great chef who started a tradition of serving free Tuesday evening community meals. He also helped us regroup after the old church burned down on Pentecost Sunday in 2012. Thanks to his organizational skills, he helped us build a brand new church in the same location.

At this time in the life of Walker (2020) we have another new minister, the ninth one since I began attending Walker that summer day in 1986. Her name is Katy. She is young, enthusiastic, full of fresh ideas, and very friendly and outgoing. I hope she stays our minister for many years to come.

I'm really glad I found the Walker community almost 24 years ago. They've become my extended family. I've made many good friends there, taken part in life-changing activities like the men's breakfast group, spiritual life group, meditation group, wisdom circle, and many others. At Walker I've also been able to express myself creatively through music, creative writing, and acting in their Christmas and Easter pageants. I've gained confidence by hosting the monthly Open Stage, as well as organizing many concerts and other events. My life has been profoundly enriched by my participation in the Walker community.

You can purchase additional copies of this memoir by
sending a check or money order for $17 per copy (includes s&h)
to Tony Wentersdorf, 1350 Nicollet Mall #607, Minneapolis, MN 55403.
Tel: 612-872-0233. Or you can visit my Facebook page..